Routledge Revivals

The Economic Growth Controversy

Is economic growth desirable? Possible? Necessary? The distinguished social scientists represented in this collection give conflicting answers, resulting in a lively debate on the costs and benefits of growth in the developed and developing countries. This volume, first published in 1973, contains proceedings of a Conference on the Limits to Growth, held at the Center for Social Research, Lehigh University, October 1972. This book will be of interest to students of economics.

T0300078

The Economic Growth Controversy

Edited by
Andrew Weintraub, Eli Schwartz,
J. Richard Aronson

First published in 1973
by International Arts and Sciences Press, Inc.

This edition first published in 2017 by Routledge
2 Park Square, Milton Park, Abingdon, Oxon, OX14 4RN
and by Routledge
711 Third Avenue, New York, NY 10017

Routledge is an imprint of the Taylor & Francis Group, an informa business

© 1973 International Arts and Sciences Press, Inc.

Publisher's Note
The publisher has gone to great lengths to ensure the quality of this reprint but points out that some imperfections in the original copies may be apparent.

Disclaimer
The publisher has made every effort to trace copyright holders and welcomes correspondence from those they have been unable to contact.

A Library of Congress record exists under LC control number: 73075076

ISBN 13: 978-1-138-93725-3 (hbk)
ISBN 13: 978-1-315-11288-6 (ebk)
ISBN 13: 978-1-138-93727-7 (pbk)

The Economic Growth Controversy

Edited by Andrew Weintraub, Eli Schwartz, J. Richard Aronson

Preface

THIS VOLUME contains proceedings of a symposium held at Lehigh University in Bethlehem, Pennsylvania, on October 17-19, 1972, under the auspices of the Center for Social Research and the Department of Economics. The original idea for the conference arose during a conversation with Jack K. Busby, who, as president of the Pennsylvania Power and Light Company (PP&L), is extremely aware of and concerned about the energy crisis and its role as a symptom of the broader problems surrounding the economic growth controversy.

With the financial backing of the Pennsylvania Power and Light Company, and the moral support of Messrs. Busby and George Wallace, economist and Director of Public Affairs at PP&L, we were able to invite scholars and students, educators, businessmen, and government officials to Lehigh for three days of intensive discussions about the problems of economic growth. The opinions expressed in these proceedings do not, of course, necessarily reflect those of PP&L or of Lehigh University.

The importance of the question, the intellectual distinction of the conference speakers and discussants, and the clarity and quality of their contributions should make this volume a significant contribution to public policy analysis. We hope that its contents will stimulate more research and contribute to a better understanding of a set of problems that may be the most challenging that mankind has ever faced.

ELI SCHWARTZ
J. RICHARD ARONSON
ANDREW WEINTRAUB

Contributors

LINCOLN H. DAY
Chief, Demographic and Social Statistics Branch
United Nations

ABRAHAM GERBER
National Economic Research Associates, Inc.

MARSHALL I. GOLDMAN
Department of Economics
Wellesley College
Russian Research Center, Harvard University

MELVIN KRANZBERG
Department of Social Science
Georgia Institute of Technology

E. J. MISHAN
Department of Economics
London School of Economics and Political Science

W. E. SCHIESSER
Computer Center and Department of
Chemical Engineering
Lehigh University

S. FRED SINGER
Department of Environmental Science
University of Virginia

Contributors

ROBERT M. SOLOW
Department of Economics
Massachusetts Institute of Technology

LESTER THUROW
Department of Economics
Massachusetts Institute of Technology

DAVID AMIDON
Center for Social Research
Lehigh University

JAY ANDERSON
Department of Chemistry
Bryn Mawr College
The Club of Rome Study Group

BARRY R. CHISWICK
Department of Economics
Queens College of the City University of New York
National Bureau of Economic Research

JOEL DARMSTADTER
Resources for the Future

RICHARD A. EASTERLIN
Department of Economics
University of Pennsylvania

FINN B. JENSEN
Department of Economics
Lehigh University

SIMON ROTTENBERG
Department of Economics
University of Massachusetts

Contents

continued

Introduction

THE RECENT BOOK *The Limits to Growth*[1] (a
product of the Club of Rome's Project on the Predicament of Mankind) has stimulated an urgent reconsid-
eration of the Malthusian prognosis. The book contains
a computer model constructed by a group of engineers
and physical scientists at Massachusetts Institute of
Technology that purports to show that, unless population growth and economic growth are halted immediately, population expansion and resource depletion will
produce a precipitous collapse of the world's economic
and environmental systems.

There have been strong reactions to this scenario. Many economists have pointed out that the hy-
potheses and assumptions used to construct the basic
Club of Rome model are unrealistic and neglectful of
basic economics. Some claim that the proponents of
zero growth may have so overstated their case that the
real dangers of mindless growth will be overlooked.

To most economists, the growth path projected
by the Club of Rome model is suspect. The picture is one
of unremitting growth up to a point and then sudden
collapse, as depicted in Figure 1. However, most economic-growth paths visualize something like that depicted in Figure 2.

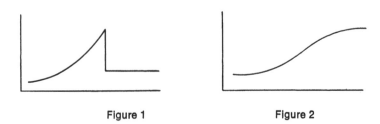

Figure 1   Figure 2

Figure 2 illustrates a growth path which accelerates to a point and then grows at a positive, but slowing, rate thereafter. This is not a pure aesthetic construct. It is a result of the economic assumption that as present income and wealth rise, the future (that is, future utility) is held in higher esteem. This means that after a certain level is reached, there will be a slowdown in the use of current resources in favor of times to come. This idea is contained in the much-discussed economic concept of the discount rate (i.e., the interest rate used in the denominator as a capitalization rate for future returns). As wealth and capital accumulate, the interest rate should fall. The lower the social discount rate, the slower will be the exploitation rate of existing resources.

The rate of technological progress may be a significant variable affecting the rate of resource use. Technology is capable of more than just turning out additional physical goods; it can be turned to recycling existing stocks, to retrieving existing waste, and to reversing, or at least halting, pollution.

The growth path depends heavily on the signals given out by the economic system. As increasing relative scarcity raises the prices of raw materials and the value of an unspoiled environment, the most profitable use of technology may be in recycling or in the conservation of natural resources. This could push the limit to growth further into the future.

Moreover, the proposal that the rate of growth in Gross National Product (GNP) be reduced does not necessarily imply a reduction in *per capita* GNP. Indeed, if the rate of population growth fell more than the proportionate fall in the rate of GNP growth, the result would be increased per capita GNP. There would also be a reduction in the rate of use of nonrenewable resources. Many who advocate a slowdown in GNP growth may still hope to promote some growth in *per capita* GNP. However, the extreme "zero growth" advocate may hope to reduce not only the rate of growth of GNP but even the absolute level of GNP.

Separating hysteria from truth is a difficult task, but the questions raised by the Club of Rome report deserve recognition and some serious thought. What is the optimal rate of economic growth? What definition of growth is to be attacked? Should actions be taken to curb growth here and now? If so, what are the proper actions? How do we deal with the more specific problems posed within the growth-no-growth framework? Can technological progress provide for the future? Is there an optimal population size? How would a no-growth policy affect the incomes of disadvantaged groups? Will the available energy supply limit growth? What are the growth problems of other nations? How would individuals adjust to a no-growth policy?

In an effort to focus on the problem, Lehigh University's Center for Social Research and Department of Economics organized a symposium on "The Economic Growth Controversy."

The word "symposium" in the ancient Greek means "getting together for feasting, drinking, and conversation." The modern meaning is "a conference for the discussion of a particular subject." Although at times our Symposium on the Economic Growth Controversy seemed to verge more to the classical than the modern definition, both purposes were served. The atmosphere was spirited, the intellectual exchange was of the highest caliber, and the participants, upon leaving, were generally satisfied for having been heard by and having listened to both their friends and intellectual opposites in the argument. At the end everyone left with a better understanding of the opposing points of view, and, what is more significant, with general agreement on the nature of the issues, if not their resolution. The consensus seemed to compress the issues into three major questions:

1. Is continued growth possible?
2. Is continued growth necessary?
3. Is continued growth desirable, i.e., is it needed to make people "happy"?

The first of these issues seems, at first, to be a fairly straightforward question, one that could be approached through positive scientific analysis. Theoretically, aside from problems of measurement, if we knew the extent of the world's stock of resources and the potential for growth in the efficiency of their use, if we had data on recycling possibilities and data on birth and death rates, we could estimate the horizon to which economic growth could continue. In fact, within its possibly limited assumptions, this is just what the model contained in *The Limits to Growth* attempts to do. Although some of the participants at the symposium questioned the methods of the computer model as well as the results which it yielded, all seemed to agree that there may be some limit to aggregate growth. The basic argument centered around when and how this limit will be reached. In seventy years, as *The Limits to Growth* predicts? Two hundred years? Sooner? Later? Will the growth horizon be approached slowly and asymptotically or at an accelerated rate followed by a violent collapse, as predicted by the Club of Rome study group?

The answer partly depends on the rate of growth that is actually attained. Obviously, all other things equal, the higher the rate of growth, the sooner we may use up our nonrenewable resources and the sooner the limit to or the slowdown of growth is reached.

Insofar as the rate of growth can be influenced by policy, it is a function of the social and political need or the desire to provide more goods and services per capita. The issues of the possibility, necessity, and desirability of growth are inextricably related to one another. One cannot divorce the problems of growth from the prevailing mores and the social, legal, and economic institutions of society. Thus "moral philosophy" may be as appropriate a subject heading as "economics" for the dialogue that follows.

Note

[1] D. H. Meadows, D. L. Meadows, J. Randers, and W. W. Behrens (New York: Universe Books, 1972).

The Economic
Growth
Controversy

1 | Growth and antigrowth: what are the issues?

E. J. MISHAN

THE DEBATE on the growth-antigrowth theme has become a fashionable pastime over the last five years. And since its continued enjoyment must depend to a large extent on its inconclusiveness, it would be boorish as well as presumptuous to propose that we try to reach a settled conclusion. Not that I think there is much danger of that happening, however. The reverse is rather to be feared: that the present enjoyment in witnessing the continual conflicts of opinion will become marred by a growing sense of frustration—not so much a frustration at being unable to reach a firm conclusion as a frustration arising from repeated failure to organize our thoughts on the subject and to acquire perspective.

If I interpret the public mood rightly, the time has come to steer the debate away from rhetorical appeals and toward more direct confrontation—less bark and more bite is in order. I propose, therefore, that we define the issues more carefully than hitherto and, in the light of these defined issues, lay down the ground rules for a more searching investigation.

The physical possibility of sustained growth

There are two aspects to the debate that may be treated separately, though they will become linked in any policy conclusion: first, whether continued economic growth is physically possible and, second, whether it is desirable.

Consider the physical possibility first. Obviously, we cannot begin without agreeing on some standard of measurement for economic growth. Are we to include population growth? Should GNP, or some variant of GNP, be used? What other indicators are there? Are we to include leisure?

There is another set of questions: Are we concerned with the economic growth of the world as a whole, or are we to confine ourselves to particular areas? And if the latter, are we to make any special assumptions about developments in the rest of the world?

Having agreed, let us suppose, to answers to these two sets of questions, we must then recognize that there exists a virtually unlimited number of possible paths of growth. If we were to consider the world as a whole, one in which human population was stabilized at, say, six billion people, we might discover—if we could foresee all major technological developments—that an average rate of growth of, say, 4 percent per annum would entail a collapse of civilization in 50 years' time, whereas an overall rate of growth of 2 percent per annum could be maintained for 200 years. Alternatively, we could generate a growth path that begins climbing steeply, only to taper off in a generation or so, after which it could continue at a low rate for centuries. Or we might discover that a 3 percent growth rate could be maintained almost indefinitely provided that it was concentrated in certain geographical areas, or provided that only certain types of technology were utilized, or provided a number of consumer services and gadgetry were scrapped.

I range over these hypothetical possibilities partly in order to uncover our woeful ignorance. We cannot, of course, foresee all major scientific and technological developments over the next few decades, much less over the next century, and therefore we cannot hope to project the range of alternative growth profiles over the future for any group of countries or for the world at large. Perforce, we must for a long time remain content to speculate about less fanciful questions such as whether the world as a whole—assuming its population growth tends to decline so as to stabilize after a given number of years—can continue to maintain a rate of economic growth of, say, 2 to 3 percent over the foreseeable future.

The question of method

The question of method would seem at first to be a fairly straightforward one around which we might profitably reflect, but there are already two questions to be settled before we can give rein to our imagination. Both refer to institutional and political developments.

First, to put the question in terms of whether the world *can* continue to maintain a 2 to 3 percent growth rate is to transform it into a question about technological possibilities. It might well be that GNP, as conventionally measured, would be perceived to grow at this rate of 2 to 3 percent per annum *provided* that all resources were properly allocated, which means that all productive services would be, in some sense, correctly priced. *Uneconomic* pollution of air, water, etc., would therefore be prevented. Indeed, an ideal allocation might require—in a broader context, and in the absence of all institutions devoted to persuading us to consume more—that all, or nearly all, productivity gains be used to increase leisure. This would imply that "real" goods per capita (other than leisure) would not grow, or would grow very little, over time. This resultant "constant-physical-product" economic growth is obviously very much easier to maintain over time than the conventional increasing-physical-product growth, especially where the allocation is so imperfect that pollutants continue to mount.

But are we entitled to make this assumption if there is not, in fact, much likelihood that allocative wisdom will prevail under existing economic and political institutions? True, the question of what *can* be done, of what is technically and economically feasible, is of academic importance. It is useful for informing policy. But if we are interested in the actual prospects for the continuation of, say, a 2 to 3 percent rate of growth into the future, we have to speculate *also* about what changes, if any, in political and economic institutions are likely to be brought about by changes in public attitudes. We have to ask that hard-nosed question: Is it realistic to expect this or that development in the foreseeable future?

Second, asking the question whether the world *can*, in a technical sense, maintain this 2 to 3 percent growth rate for a longish period is to abstract also from present dangers that appear increasingly to threaten human survival. To list some of them:

1) the threat of ecological catastrophe resulting from larger-scale and more ruthless interference in the biosphere;

2) the threat of genetic calamity arising from increased radiation, and from thousands of new chemicals coming onto the market each year, about whose long-run effects, singly or in combination, we know practically nothing;[1]

3) the increased danger of epidemics, or "pandemics," owing to increased travel opportunities;

4) the threat to human survival arising from the growth of more resistant pests and viruses in response to more powerful drugs;

5) the danger of a nuclear Armageddon, or of annihilation by more horrible means, as an increasing number of the smaller countries, often headed by fanatics, come to possess the secrets of thermonuclear destruction and biological warfare;

6) the danger that the postwar trend toward increasing blackmail, violence, crime, and corruption—a product also of the erosion, in the West, of notions of patriotism, civic virtue, and standards of right and wrong—will plunge society into anarchy (from which it might be saved only by the most repressive tyranny);

7) the threat of internecine warfare, especially in poorer areas, because of continued frustration of expectations—expectations aggravated by growth in travel, communications, and mass media;

8) the conflicts that may soon arise from the growth in illegal immigration from poor to rich countries.

Again, we are constrained to ask whether we should abstract from these very real threats to our civilization, or to our survival, in appraising the prospects for sustained future economic growth. It is hardly to be doubted that each of these threats has arisen from economic and technological growth, and that each will be further aggravated by economic and technological growth in the future. Though what has happened in the past can be regarded as irrelevant to the question of whether we can, or will, continue to grow in the future, the question of the physical possibility of continued growth is couched in terms of whether *in fact* we shall be able to grow. If so, we can hardly exclude from a consideration of this eventuality the risk of those events which, should they occur, would cripple human society or blot it out completely.

Let me add in passing that these dire possibilities are not to be exorcised by jeers of "doomsdayism." True, history is littered with false prophecies, but not only pessimistic ones. "Prosperity" Robinson, the British statesman who in 1827 assured his countrymen that they were entering an era of unprecedented prosperity, lived on to witness an unprecedented depression that did not lift until about 1844. And no economist is likely to forget President Hoover's cheerful news in 1929 that prosperity was "just around the corner." But the fact that there have been and still are millennial prophecies allows us to infer nothing about the future. Calling "Wolf!" frequently and mistakenly does not mean that wolves do not exist. The dangers that exist today, some of which I listed above, are *not* imaginary. Scholars may differ about their magnitudes, and about the risks or likelihoods of their occurring, but there is general agreement among them that nothing comparable to such dangers existed at the beginning of the century and, as far as I know, none has argued that the dangers are receding.

Nonetheless, having taken due note of them, I am prepared, for the sake of argument, to turn away from these very real dangers and to consider the possibility of sustained economic growth in their assumed absence.

Technology, the crucial variable

Suppose, then, that we can reasonably anticipate a stable world population in the foreseeable future and that the question we have to face is whether, irrespective of the distribution of future world product, an average rate of growth per capita of *physical* product, comparable to that "enjoyed" in the postwar period, can be maintained for the next few centuries *in the absence of* the dangers listed above. What should we have to know in order to tackle such a question?

Knowledge of existing reserves of materials

chiefly used in modern industry is clearly not enough. We already have rough estimates of the remaining reserves of coal, oil (for varying degrees of accessibility), and a large number of metals. And even if they turn out to be underestimates by as much as a factor of two or three or more, it will make little difference to the number of years required to exhaust them at current rates of depletion. If, for example, world oil consumption continues to increase at a rate of about 10 percent per annum, known reserves (including projected future discoveries) should be exhausted in about two decades. Even if reserves turn out to be as much as four times as large as currently estimated, we could keep going only for another fourteen years. And if they were eight times as large, which is hardly possible, we could keep going for another two decades.

I think there is general agreement that we cannot continue to mine a wide range of primary materials *at current rates* for much longer than the end of the century.

Knowledge of economics is not enough either. Economists continue to remind us, unnecessarily perhaps, that as a resource becomes more scarce, its price rises, and, as a result, it is used less intensively. If there is a famine in some part of Asia, grain prices will rise accordingly—though I doubt whether this classical example of the proper functioning of the price mechanism will afford the starving natives much consolation. More generally, and in the absence of other events, a rise in the prices of depleting resources acts to reduce living standards through a rise in the cost of living at some rate that depends on physical factors and on economic institutions. True, the rise in the price of a depleting resource is also expected to induce enterprises to switch to substitutes, thus cushioning the rise in prices of those products that depend heavily on such resources. And it must be admitted that in the textbook constructs these substitutes are unfailingly on tap. Yet in the world in which we live, we cannot be so sure that our luck in the past will continue to hold. Indeed, it may be unreasonable to expect our luck in discovering close substitutes in the past to continue when all but a few of today's "essential" metals will, if trends continue, be exhausted within fifty years. At current rates of usage, all known reserves of silver, gold, copper, lead, platinum, tin, and zinc will be used up within twenty years. There is no historical experience of man being able to find substitutes simultaneously for so large a group of important materials.

We may reasonably conclude that, *were there to be no technological innovation in the future,* then we simply would not be able to continue to grow indefinitely. The earth and its resources are finite, all too finite, and our continued consumption of them on an ever larger scale must eventually exhaust them. The only question would be when. And the answers (in the absence of technology) would all seem to fall within the next half century.

The crucial variable in all optimistic forecasts and in all declarations of faith is technological innovation. We read of existing technical possibilities that are likely to be translated into commercial processes or products. We read also of current technological advances, of being close to a number of "exciting" developments or "breakthroughs," particularly in the field of energy, and we are prone to take heart. For do we not have behind us a couple of hundred years of remarkable scientific success and technological achievement? Surely this trend must continue as the base of our knowledge expands.

Fact or fantasy?

To a layman like myself, it is hard to distinguish in these reports—and not all are optimistic—between the elements of fact and fantasy, of reasonable expectation and wild hope. Living in a world that is today being transformed before our eyes by new applications of science, we find it hard to remain skeptical about scientific claims that it will soon be possible to release unlimited supplies of energy from granite or water. For there is today an almost irresistible presumption in favor of scientific capability. If it merely sounds possible, the layman is ready to believe it will happen. Thus we are ready to accept the idea of a vast proliferation of nuclear power plants over the earth, with problems of space solved and with radiation and heat hazards all kept well under control.

If we are not to run out of materials, however, we shall have to recycle them, so we are ready to imagine also that technology will discover increasingly more efficient (low loss) and inexpensive ways of doing this. And though finite amounts of materials must ultimately limit the period of continued expansion, by switching over time from the consumption of products to the consumption of services, we may find it possible to prolong the period of continued economic growth for hundreds of years.

As for food supplies, the optimistic view is that the problem can be solved by intensive monoculture utilizing large tracts of land and large amounts of chemical fertilizers and pesticides—the methods of the so-called Green Revolution. We are to suppose also that technology will respond promptly and successfully to adverse short- and long-term ecological repercussions associated with modern "engineering" methods of agriculture, and we are to ignore the social consequences of such agrotechnology on the economy of the hundreds of thousands of Asian villages, and the urban problems that follow the disruption of traditional ways of life.

I do not want to sound too cynical. It may all be

wonderfully possible, or we may all be wonderfully lucky. I would simply affirm that there is room for legitimate doubt.

The advance of technology in the West over the past 200 years might well be attributable to especially favorable circumstances. Certainly there was no problem up to the present of limits to the assimilative capacity of the biosphere. Nor was there a problem of the availability of cheap fossil fuels. As for scientific progress, we may be running into diminishing returns to scale of research —partly because of an incipient breakdown in communication among an expanding array of narrowly focused specialists. Moreover, it might well be the case that there are no solutions to a number of problems that scientists are working on. It may be that the things we want to be able to do just cannot, in the nature of things, ever be done—though it may take us decades to realize this. Finally, it is possible—alas, more than possible—that, should we succeed in wresting some of nature's closest secrets from her breast, we shall live to wish we had not.

So we may well persist in our doubts, and ask again: How sure can we be that soon we shall be able to release unlimited amounts of energy without undue danger? How sure can we be that soon we shall be able to recycle, cheaply and without waste, a wide range of raw materials? What of the limits of space on increasing earth travel? And, not least, what of the limits of time on rising levels of consumption?

A sustained per capita growth rate of 3 percent per annum implies that the average income in 150 years will be about 100 times as large as the average income today, and 10,000 times as large in another 150 years. Just contemplate the amounts of energy and materials required to meet such fantastic standards! Just what shape will expenditures of this magnitude take? And how on earth (literally) will a person manage to absorb it?

The desirability of sustained economic growth

Assuming that per capita growth could be maintained indefinitely at current rates, we now ask whether it is desirable. The question is still a bit vague, however, and lends itself to a number of interpretations.

1. We might, for example, be asking the question: Are we getting our money's worth from the rising tide of affluence? If so, the answer is surely no. Even the most conservative economist would agree that a little political initiative would rid us of a lot of unnecessary spillovers. Eighteenth-century believers in progress would be astounded at our technological capabilities, and they would be dismayed at what we have done with them. How could we justify the sheer ugliness and abandon of our cities, their endless clamor, litter, stench, tawdriness, and desolation? Let us concede that we could have used our enormous wealth to create more sensible ways of living, and pass on to other possible interpretations of the question.

2. We might want to compare the quality or wholesomeness of life today with that of bygone ages. And growthmen are ever quick for such comparisons. Yet the comparisons they make are unfair in several ways. First, they use what little history they know to select the bleaker periods of the past: "the dark satanic mills" and other grim features of the earlier part of the Industrial Revolution, which is a much-favored point of reference, or the ancient slave economies of the East, or the imaginary life of an early caveman, "nasty, brutish, and short."

Second, they accent those aspects of life which, precisely because of rising affluence and indiscriminate consumerism, have assumed disproportionate importance in our lives—hygiene, longevity, youthfulness, mobility, instant entertainment, self-indulgence, effort-avoidance. Inadvertently, they also neglect to stress the features that were common to all preindustrial ages, the (by our standards) inordinate number of holidays and holy days, the lack of a clear distinction between work and living, and a vaster sense of time and space (owing to slow travel, slow news, and few timepieces). There were also the great myths that gave hope of life beyond the grave, a more settled way of life, a greater joy in nature, easy access to the countryside—to clean air, to lakes, rivers, quiet fields, and woodlands.[2]

Third, in comparing the quality of life in different periods of history, the notion of some average sort of life has to be abandoned. In all ages, including our own, there are rich and poor, fortunate and unfortunate, and the proportions of these can vary from place to place and from one age to another. A historian may be able to pick out certain periods, over the last 5,000 years, during which, for certain groups in particular parts of the world, life appeared to be good and wholesome, while for a fair proportion of the remainder, it was not burdensome.[3] Such comparisons are to some extent subjective and inconclusive, though there may be more agreement among historians on some periods and places than on others. I doubt, however, whether many historians would agree to the use of GNP as a historical yardstick of well-being, and to conclude, therefore, that life today is transparently happier than it ever was before.

3. We might more reasonably be asking if life is becoming more enjoyable, or if we are becoming better people, or more contented people, as a consequence of economic growth. Bearing in mind the facts of human nature, we could reflect on current economic and social developments in particular areas in order to obtain clues about the extent to which the modes of living they give rise to accord with, or conflict with, men's biological and

psychic needs. And by speculating about technological and economic developments over the foreseeable future, we can debate whether, on balance, we are likely to be better people, or more contented people, over the next few decades.

This seems to me to be the more promising area of inquiry, and the one to which I suggest we direct our attention.

Obviously, we cannot *prove* propositions about the decline in social welfare as one can prove, for example, that a significant rise in the price of beef, *ceteris paribus,* will cause a fall in the maximum amount of beef that people are willing to buy. In debating social welfare, subjective judgments are required—judgments of fact and possibly also judgments of value.

I say *possibly* judgments of value because they could be avoided. To illustrate with an extreme example: I may assert that murder is "wrong." If you agree with me, then we share the same value or ethic in this respect. If, however, you do not agree with me, I could try to persuade you. I could quote the golden rule. I could describe the apprehension of honest men if murderers went unpunished. I could talk of the pity of blotting out the life of an innocent man. I could depict the grief of his family and the loss suffered by the community. And thus by an appeal to your imagination, to your feelings and conscience—a product of instinct, education, social environment, and emotional experience—I might finally elicit your assent to the proposition that it is wrong to murder.

I could, however, try another tack. Though again I would rouse your imagination by describing the likely consequences of regarding murder as an acceptable form of conduct—the sorrow of the victim's family, the fears that might come to dominate so tolerant a society, the time and effort people would have to spend in attempting to protect themselves—I would not try to persuade you to agree that murder is wrong. I merely would suggest that such consequences are not compatible with the good life, at least not with a happy life. If you agree with me that a murder-permissive society is likely to result in a decline in people's experienced happiness, then you are subscribing to a judgment of *fact*.

It is unnecessary to remark that there can be close connections between judgments of facts and judgments of values. But in the sort of debate in which we are immersed, there are advantages in emphasizing the distinction. In any event, the kinds of judgment found in many of the arguments that follow are chiefly, perhaps wholly, judgments of fact. These judgments are invoked in detecting consequences, in gauging the likelihood of their occurrence, and in appraising their impact on people's well-being. Included also are judgments about the nature of people's value judgments. And although both kinds of judgment are necessarily subjective—that is, they cannot be proved "scientifically"—it does not follow that they cannot be regarded as dependable guides to action. Not all judgments command equal respect or equal assent. Nor should they. The belief that the music of the Beatles will outlast that of Beethoven (which I assure you is held by some of the young) is not, I submit, an intelligent belief, and I would not waste my time arguing about it. Nor, again, is the view that "push-penny is as good as Pushkin," or that the *Adventures of Superman* provides as much authentic human experience as Tolstoy's *War and Peace,* worth disputing. Certainly if society ever abandoned itself to such indiscriminate tolerance, literature would have no place in the curricula of our schools and universities.

In this connection, I will remind you also that we are restricting our attention to the affluent societies of the West[4] in which there is still a fair consensus of opinion and some common beliefs about the constituents of the good life. I should also remind you that, when judging the past or envisioning the future, we must not unquestioningly attribute *all* events and *all* developments to economic and technological growth. Some significant events, good or bad, may have quite tenuous links with economic and technological growth, though, indeed, they may be mitigated or aggravated by them. But while exercising some scruples in this regard, we must not go so far as to omit factors that could be decisive simply because a statistical relationship has not been satisfactorily established or is unlikely to be.[5]

What is not agenda

Of the odd assortment of arguments that come up in this debate, a number are quite definitely "nonstarters." We can save time and heat by recognizing some of them before going any further.

1. There is, first, the frequent statement that, like science, technology itself—the main force behind current economic growth—is neutral: one cannot, therefore, associate it with good or evil attributes. "It all depends on how man uses it."

This is not helpful. In the first place, let us not talk of "man," a singular embodiment of heroic qualities. Let us talk of men as they emerge from history, organized into nation-states, ideologically aligned and perpetually struggling for advantage. While recognizing the dedication of some, and the sterling qualities of many, there is no lack of historical incident to illustrate also their imprudence, folly, corruptibility, and iniquity. Yet it is to this society of imperfect beings and institutions that science vouchsafes its discoveries and translates their potential into technology. If, in such a society, science is a power for good, it is also a power for evil. Science as an institution, and scientists individually, cannot reasonably absolve themselves of the uses made of their discoveries in an unsteady equilibrium of nation-states whose citizens are impelled by greed and ambition.[6]

Thus, the *potential* of science and technology for good (or evil) is not the issue. Their *actual* effects are. Intelligent conjecture about the future presupposes some knowledge of the existing power and reach of modern science, and also some idea of the scientific developments over the foreseeable future, from which we can speculate about some of the more likely consequences on our lives and character, bearing in mind the limitations of men and the driving forces of modern institutions, economic and political. Only in this way can we rightly appraise the contributions that science and technology have made, and are likely to make, to the human condition.

2. A related response, that of invoking a "challenge" to man to "face the future" or to "be worthy of his destiny," and other such rhetoric, must also go off the board. Otherwise, we shall find ourselves handling a two-headed penny. For wherever science and technology can be seen to have caused trouble or created social problems, the technocrats exclaim "challenge," and perceive an immediate need for more technology. But wherever they appear to have had benign consequences, why, there is clear proof of the blessings they confer on humankind. Again, then, we must strive impartially to appraise their record and their future prospects, although always alert to the possibility that some of the problems inflicted upon us by the advance of technology can also be solved by using less of the existing technology.

3. Nor is it, for similar reasons, legitimate to argue that economic growth *per se* is above reproach, that economic growth *can* be good. A well-known economist— I admit it with reluctance—judiciously defended economic growth on the grounds that although it could be

bad in some circumstances, it could also be good, and that whereas it could be too fast, it could also be too slow. Inevitably, he concluded that we should seek the "optimal," just-right, rate of growth. This sort of reasoning is but a lapse into tautologies. I do not doubt that the same economist would wish to persuade us that, if purged of all externalities, Hell itself would be a comfortable place in which to live.

One can imagine some distillation of economic growth, some essence purified of all harmful external effects, which—when the term "external effect" is defined broadly enough—cannot fail to result in ideal human progress. But such flights of inspiration offer no plausible picture of the future and no guide to action. Economists all know that a narrow range of adverse spillovers can beneficially be reduced given some political initiative and effort. These spillovers include air and water pollution, noise, congestion, ugliness, and tourist blight. Yet this is not at all to the point. In judging the quality of life over the last two decades, we obviously *cannot* abstract from the brute facts of expanding pollution. So, also, in debating the foreseeable future, it is not the potential ideal that economists believe they could realize, not the brave words of government officials or corporation executives, that are agenda, but the political likelihood of significant reductions being made over the next two decades in each of the familiar forms of pollution.[7]

4. The "need" to maintain the momentum of economic growth in order to enable us to do good deeds is also not agenda. The good deeds include helping the poor and ailing, promoting high culture, and expanding higher education.[8] It is not simply that these arguments for the persistent pursuit of economic growth are quite distinct from those which turn on greater social welfare or happiness. For these arguments might win ethical support even if it were agreed that economic growth actually

entailed a decline in social welfare for the majority of people. The fact is that such worthy objectives can all be realized *without* sustained economic growth (unless by helping the poor we mean helping the have-nots in the economically backward two-thirds of the world).[9]

If it is a question of helping the indigenous poor in a variety of ways, or promoting the arts, or expanding adult education, we should first ask about the order of the sums envisaged. Will about $20 billion be enough? If not, perhaps $50 billion, or $100 billion? But the latter figure is hardly more than three years' growth of GNP at current rates. Without anyone being made worse off, it would be technically feasible to distribute another $100 billion among these good causes. If we were really extravagant, we could justify perhaps five or six years' growth at current rates, but hardly more than that. What is yet more to the point, however, we do not really have to raise the GNP of the United States to higher levels for such purposes. For with the abundance of the "demerit" goods that are produced today, with so much produced that is trivial, inane, if not inimical, we already have more than enough resources in hand to transfer resources to the production of these more meritorious goods instead.

5. And this brings us to the question of political realism in a new connection. For we have already spoken of the need for gauging the likelihood of future developments—for example, of reducing spillovers in the near future—in the light of given attitudes and institutions. The above observation, then, that some alleged good purposes of economic growth could conceivably be realized without economic growth should also, it might seem, face the question of political realism. For instance, is it likely that people today, or in the near future, would agree to a transfer of some $30 billion to $50 billion, an annual sum which would surely suffice to remove all hard-core pov-

erty from our midst? And although such sums amount to no more than 3 to 5 percent of GNP, the answer is probably no. Given the institutional constraints, it may be concluded, we can only do a little more for the poor by continuing to do a great deal more for ourselves. On such attractive terms, technocrats and businessmen are always glad to do good.

But although this conclusion follows, it does not constitute a vindication of economic growth. Quite the contrary. Recall an earlier *caveat* that, in appraising the salient features of modern society, the debate requires the presumption that they are related to economic growth. The feature in this instance—the fact that, even while there is evidence everywhere of overindulgence and almost criminal waste, the citizens of the affluent societies cannot collectively agree to curb their more extravagant expenditures so as to alleviate the wretched poverty of others of their countrymen—is surely related to the processes of economic growth. If this rather lamentable "institutional restraint" springs from an ethos that is favorable, if not essential, to economic growth, an ethos that is indeed promoted by economic growth; if, to be more explicit, the pursuit of economic growth over the years has been maintained, and will continue to be maintained, only by the priority given by individuals to self-seeking, and if that self-seeking is aggravated by the discontent generated by the system itself, then such "institutional constraints" are themselves among the more shameful products of economic growth.

In sum, by accepting current political attitudes as constraints, or "parameters," we are implicitly passing harsh judgment on the human consequences of the pursuit of economic growth.

6. Finally, in arguing that the pursuit of economic growth in the West today is causing a decline in social welfare, it is admittedly interesting, and to some

extent pertinent, to examine just how this decline in social welfare comes about under existing social institutions, in particular under liberal democracies with responsive legislatures and in competitive private enterprise economies, which supposedly enable people to make individual and collective choices. Though I have had some thoughts on this question elsewhere,[10] it is not imperative to discuss the matter here. One can quite convincingly demonstrate that Hitler led the German people into disaster without first having to explain just why they voted him into power.

It is surpassingly convenient for the professional economist to interpret people's market choices, or their economic behavior generally, as reflecting their mature judgment about what is most conducive to their happiness. But I hope he is not such a fool as really to believe it. It is also convenient for the economist to be heard championing the right of the citizen to spend his money as he wishes. And for my part, I have no objection if he prefers to sleep on a mattress stuffed with breakfast cereal. For I am not questioning his *right* to choose: I am questioning only the *consequences* of his choices. The eventual consequences, foreseen or not—and usually they are not—of individual and collective choices are an area of investigation that can be separated from the question of the political expedience in allowing people to make such choices and of their motives and promptings in making them. We can sharpen the debate by focusing only on the consequences.

Some general remarks

Having, hopefully, cleared away some of the verbal undergrowth that tends to impede the progress of this debate, we are better able to perceive the issues that can be decisive. Since we are restricting the question to whether sustained per capita growth of GNP in the West has recently promoted and is likely to promote social welfare, these issues can be divided, arbitrarily perhaps, into two categories.

In the first are the conventional array of adverse spillovers, air pollution, water pollution, solid pollution, noise, uglification of town and country, all of which have increased alarmingly since the war.[11] The question is, have they more than offset the "normal" expectations of welfare gains? Also, are such spillovers likely to continue to grow so rapidly in the future as to more than offset potential welfare gains? Again, I would emphasize that when future trends are in question, the alleged potentialities for good, the hopes and aspirations of technocrats, and political declarations of intent are *not* to count. What is required is a judgment of the likely outcomes, given the constellation of political and commercial forces.

In the second category are the remaining consequences of economic growth. How much weight is to be given to those pervasive repercussions that are less tangible and more complex than the familiar external diseconomies mentioned above? Doubtless, a lot of nervous excitement is generated by new discoveries—or "breakthroughs" as we love to call them today—and there is sure to be some initial exhilaration at possessing a new gadget or experiencing a new form of travel or sport. But these emotions have little affinity with the good life. We must turn from these frivolities to a consideration of the Faustian spirit that has taken possession of our society and allows us neither rest nor respite. Unwittingly, through the process of continually and unquestioningly adapting our style and pace of life to technological and commercial possibilities, we may be irrevocably losing traditional sources of comfort and gratification. Those most pessimistic about the future are concerned primarily with these less measurable consequences of continued economic growth.

Spillovers

It is difficult to draw a balance sheet summarizing the net welfare effects of the increased output of goods and the concomitant spillovers over the last few years. Even if we had details of all the physical data, from the hazards of chemical pesticides to rising levels of noise, from oil-fouled beaches the world over to forest-cropping and earth-stripping, we should, in a closely interdependent economic system, be faced with the almost impossible task of evaluation. My inclination is to describe what has been happening on the advancing pollution front in impressionistic terms, while taking it for granted that the balance of the argument will be restored by the unremitting efforts of commercial advertising, establishment politicians, company chairmen, and the spate of articles in our newspapers and magazines that speak loudly of the goodies we have and of goodies yet to come. Thus we can be certain that most people are kept continually aware of the manifold blessings of economic growth: fancier varieties of frozen packaged goods and new slimming tablets and vibrators; sleeker, faster automobiles and more comfortable artificial limbs; high-powered gardening implements and double soundproof windows; more thrilling television programs and more powerful psychiatric drugs; and so on.

In addition to describing the impact on our lives of these ubiquitous spillover effects,[12] the old-fashioned notion of diminishing marginal utility of goods and the increasing marginal disutility of "bads" can bear more emphasis. And not only the diminishing marginal utility of goods but the very real possibility of negative marginal utility. For one thing, choosing from an increasing variety of goods can be a tense and time-consuming process, even with impartial consumers' services that can seldom keep abreast of rapid change in products and models. For another, as Stefan Linder observes in his admirable and amusing *Harried Leisure Classes*, Americans are already becoming frantic in trying to find time to make use of all the gadgets and sports gear they feel impelled to buy. And they suffer endless frustrations simply in trying to "get away" in their automobiles to recreation centers along with millions of other Americans equally determined to get away.

Another matter needs emphasis. The incidence of a single spillover alone—be it foul air, endless traffic bedlam, noise, or fear of criminal violence[13]—can be enough to counter all the alleged gains of economic prosperity. Let a family have five television sets, four refrigerators, three cars, two yachts, a private plane, a swimming pool, and half a million dollars' worth of securities. What joy is left to its members if there is barely a moment of the day or night when their ears are not being assaulted by air and ground traffic? What enjoyment is left to a family that fears to stroll outdoors on an evening, that must take elaborate precautions against burglary, that lives in continuous anxiety lest one or another, parent or child, be kidnapped, mutilated, or murdered? A fat bag of consumer goods, an impressive list of technical achievements, can hardly compensate for any one of such ugly facts—a product of postwar affluence—that have come to blight the lives of millions of Americans, and to turn to ashes their hopes for a better future.

Finally, there is, in this connection, one super spillover effect worthy of special mention. Familiar to economists, it argues more strongly against continued economic growth if only because it is one for which the economist can propose no remedy consistent with such growth. I refer to what is known in the jargon as the *relative income hypothesis* or, more facetiously, the *Jones effect* (i.e., the keeping-up-with-the-Joneses effect).

In an affluent society, people's satisfactions, as Thorstein Veblen observed, depend not only on the innate or perceived utility of the goods they buy, but also on the status value of such goods. A more general way of putting the matter is to state that the satisfaction a person derives from his current expenditure depends not only on the goods he buys but also on the goods bought by others; not only on his own income and expenditure but on those of others. Thus, to a person in a high consumption society, it is not only his absolute income that counts but also his *relative* income, his position in the structure of incomes. In its extreme form— and as affluence rises (according to the theory) we draw closer to it—only relative income matters. A man would then prefer a 5 percent reduction in his income with a 10 percent reduction in the incomes of others to a 25 percent increase in both his income and those of others.

The more this attitude prevails—and the ethos of our society actively promotes it—the more futile is the objective of economic growth for society as a whole. For it is obvious that over time everybody cannot become relatively better off. The economist can, of course, continue to spin his optimal equations even in these conditions, but he has no means of measuring the loss in terms of utter futility. Since the extent of these wealth-dissipative effects is never measured, estimates over the last few years of increments of "real" income (or "measured economic welfare") are wholly misleading.

The less tangible consequences

To quote from Gilbert and Sullivan, "things are

never what they seem!" And we can adopt this dictum as the leitmotif in reflecting on the unmeasurable consequences of economic growth in an already wealthy society.

1. Consider the motive forces behind economic growth.

a) Has the extreme division of labor come to thwart an instinct for craftsmanship?

In preindustrial ages, there was satisfaction in fashioning the whole product from the materials of the earth, and pride in serving a community that valued excellence.

b) As Bernard Shaw remarked, "discontent is the mainspring of progress"; this discontent is writ large in the ethos of the affluent society. It is institutionalized by the agencies of Madison Avenue and hallowed by our system of higher education. If continued discontent with what they have is required to keep people buying the increasing outputs of industry, and continued discontent with their status is necessary to keep them working the machine, can we really believe that people are nonetheless happier as they absorb more goods? The secret of how to keep people running is to widen the gap between their material condition and their material expectations. That gap is a fair measure of their discontent, and it was never wider than it is today.

c) Does not the consequent struggle for status in an increasingly anonymous society become so obsessive as to cut a person off from enjoyment of the largeness of life?

d) Does not this "virtue" of motivation, or inordinate ambition, act to shrivel a person's generous impulses and to make it habitual to use other people as a means to advancement, thus unavoidably corrupting his character and his capacity for friendship?

2. Let us look at the "knowledge industry," whose products fuel the engine of economic growth. In a society that pays ritual homage to our great secular cathedrals of knowledge, the words "scientific research" are holy and scholarship is almost synonymous with saintliness. But the social consequences of the disinterested pursuit of knowledge are not all beyond dispute.

a) As indicated, the harrowing degree of specialization that results from the attempt to advance the expanding boundary of any discipline can crush the capacity of men for instinctual pleasure. Of more topical concern, perhaps, this intense specialization is making communication between scientists increasingly difficult, even though they are working in the same general field.

b) Democracy becomes more vulnerable as decisions are increasingly influenced by experts (partly because the area of government activity has been steadily expanding over the last half century under the impact of technology).

c) Some technologies we ardently wish we had never stumbled upon, and never could have: nuclear bombs, poison gas, biochemical methods of extermination.

d) The advance of scientific knowledge enhances the secular to the detriment of the sacred. One wonders if the loss of the great myths, the loss of belief in a benevolent deity, in reunion after death, has not contributed to a sense of desolation.[14] One wonders also if a code of morality can be widely accepted in a society without belief in any god or in any hereafter.

e) As historical knowledge grows, and hawk-eyed scholars find a vocation in debunking national heroes and popular legend, the pride of peoples in their common past is eroded and, along with it, their morale as well.

3. We also might want to ponder briefly some of the unexpected repercussions of a number of much-heralded inventions.

a) The automobile, in addition to producing congestion, noise, stench and visual distraction, has been chiefly responsible for the monotony, the sameness, and ugliness of vast urban areas the world over. With automobiles multiplying like the locust, swarming through every street and alley, all the mingling and gaiety once associated with the famous cities of the world have become things of the past.

b) The airplane, in addition to plunging us into an era of shrieking skies from which it is virtually impossible to escape (short of living in isolation), has been responsible for a tourist explosion that has destroyed irrevocably all the once-famed beauty spots of the Mediterranean coast.

I might add in passing that this is not the lament of an elitist. These spillovers would have occurred, under the existing commercial institutions, irrespective of the distribution of incomes. They are simply a question of numbers—too many people and too many automobiles. The chief loss will fall on future generations who are on the way to inheriting a world almost bereft of scenic beauty and grandeur.

c) Television, usually acclaimed for its limitless potential for educating, also has limitless potential for holding people inert for hours. It promotes uniformity of speech—poor and hackneyed speech at that. It exposes innocent folk to repeated doses of expert opinion and panel discussions which have the unhappy result of enabling them to see so many sides to a question that they are left in a state of stupefaction, with no further confidence in their own judgment and without convictions of any sort—ready, in short, to believe and to forget anything. Television might fairly be designated the new opiate of the people, without which they might become so acutely aware of the intolerable features of the environment in which they are submerged that they would become restless for reform.

4. We might wonder in a general way whether the unhappier consequences of commercially inspired innovations are inescapable.

a) Does not universal plenty itself breed a throw-away attitude toward things? When a child has but one doll, she tends to treat it with loving care. When she has a dozen (half of them mechanized), they become items in a collection. Gifts lose the power to move when a person has "everything" and when wealth is such that no sacrifice is entailed in giving them.[15]

b) New creature comforts sell well in affluent societies: air-conditioning, comfortable mattresses and sofas, push-button gadgets. But do they not result in boredom and loss of appetite? Was not man made to use his muscles, to struggle physically, to endure? Without struggle there is no relish; without hardship there is no enjoyment of ease—and without pain there is no love. In seeking the devices of instant gratifications purveyed by modern enterprise, and popular fashion, men cut themselves off from the medley of experiences that make them human.

c) Technology, as a form of compulsive systematization, has begun to edge itself into every niche of what used to be our private lives and secret feelings. Methods for success, for "optimizing" in sex, are taught now by tape and manual. Techniques for love, friendship, fervor, sarcasm, surrender, repartee, fantasy, impulse, laughter are all imparted to the buyer of the booklet or tape or to the enrollee in the course. Already the social science "experts" have started to introduce such matters as part of "life adjustment" courses at schools. Soon there may be no corner into which a person might crouch and call his own. He will become a part of a world of mime and mimicry, where feelings are engineered, where spontaneity is rehearsed, and no untutored emotion is left to well up within him. Imagine a world in which all the love letters we receive are copies from models, and in which the love we experience from childhood onward has all been studied as a technique.[16]

d) Consumer innovations over the recent past and foreseeable future appear to be largely labor-saving, among them innovations for reducing the dependence of people on others—or rather, for transferring their dependence on other human beings to dependence on the machine. Yet is it not true that it is through this human interdependence that affection habitually flows? Packaged and precooked foods save the time of the busy housewife. But when a woman cooks for her man or her family, is it only a chore? Is there not also some instinctual (if not biological) satisfaction in feeding her man or children, a symbolic giving of herself to them, an act of tenderness and affirmation?

Children's records or children's television programs can dispense with Mother's or Father's bedtime storytelling, but does not the child who leans against his parent's breast and listens as the tale is gently unfolded enjoy and share a richer experience?

At the flick of a finger, we can flood the room with orchestral music perfectly executed, a delight to the ear if we did not have so much of it on such easy terms that inattentively we hum snatches while we eat, talk, read, and wash dishes. But before the turn of the century, when the music a man enjoyed might depend on his wife's skill at the pianoforte or on his daughter's singing, was there not also some quiet joy flowing between them?

It is sobering to wonder seriously if more and

more of what is innately trivial is being gained at a cost of more and more of what is innately valuable. Given the fact that the machine is incomparably more efficient, can its efficiency in yielding services compensate for the inevitable loss of authentic human experience? Can we reasonably expect that the technological innovations of the future will have a more humanizing effect?

Surely it is more likely that the main thrust of product innovation associated with economic growth in already wealthy countries will act over time to diminish the opportunities for direct communication between people inasmuch as it seeks overtly to reduce their need of the direct services of other human beings. Personal contacts necessarily decline with the spread of more efficient labor-saving devices. They have already declined with the spread of supermarkets, cafeterias, and vending machines, with the spread of transistors and television sets, and, of course, the automobile. And they will continue to decline with the trend toward computerization in offices and factories, toward patient-monitoring machines and computer-diagnoses in hospitals, toward closed-circuit television instruction, automated libraries, and teaching machines.

Thus the compulsive search for efficiency, directed in the main toward innovations that save effort and time, must continue to produce for us yet more elegant instruments for our mutual estrangement. The unavoidable consequence is a gradual drying up of the direct flow of sympathy and affectionate communication between people, a thinness of their emotional lives, and, therefore, despite the proliferation of glittering baubles, a persistent sense of frustration.

5. Finally, we might ask if the things commonly associated with the good life—a more settled way of living, more margin, a greater sense of ease and space, an environment of natural beauty and architectural dignity, a rehabilitation of norms of prosperity and taste—

can ever be realized by affluent societies straining eternally to woo the consumer with ever more outlandish and expendable gadgetry and seeking eternally for faster economic growth.

And what of the attributes by which men live? If it is conceded that, once subsistence levels have been passed (and they have in the West), the sources of men's more enduring satisfactions spring from mutual trust and affection, from sharing joy and sorrow, from giving and accepting love, from open-hearted companionship and laughter; if it is further conceded that in a civilized society the joy of living is augmented primarily by the sense of wonder inspired by the unfolding of nature, by the perception of beauty inspired by great art, and by the renewal of faith and hope inspired by the heroic and the good—if this much is conceded, is it possible to believe also that unremitting attempts to harness the greater part of men's energies and ingenuity to the task of amassing an ever greater assortment of material possessions can add much to people's happiness? Can they add more than they subtract? Can they add anything?

Even if we ignore the darker side of economic growth, we have already remarked that, as affluence increases, the Jones effect acts to dissipate any sense of improved well-being for society as a whole, which, in effect, is gulled into struggling on, accumulating, destroying, innovating, to no intelligent purpose. But, of course, we cannot possibly ignore those several consequences of economic growth that, in the very nature of the growth process, corrode the chief sources of human happiness. Inevitably, then, we conclude that the growth game is not worth the candle. And the answer to the question of whether continued economic growth in the West brings us any closer to the good life cannot be other than a resounding No.

Notes

[1] We were lucky to discover the mutative effects of Thalidomide in time. We might not be so lucky next time, if only because the genetic effects of other drugs will take much longer before they are recognized — by which time it might be too late.

[2] In preindustrial civilizations, according to Jacques Ellul, the time given to the use of techniques was short compared with the leisure time devoted to sleep, conversation, games, and meditation.

For primitive man and historical man, work as such was *not* a virtue. It was better not to consume than to work hard. Thus man worked as little as possible and was content with restricted consumption.

Today, comfort means easy chairs, foam rubber mattresses, bathrooms, air-conditioning, washing machines, etc. The chief concern is to avoid physical effort, and therefore we become more dependent upon the machine.

According to Giedion (quoted by Ellul), men of the Middle Ages were also concerned with comfort. But for them comfort represented a moral and aesthetic order. Space was the primary element. Men sought open spaces and large rooms. They did not care if the chairs were hard or the rooms ill-heated. What mattered was proportion and the materials used.

[3] For the recent history of England, I should be inclined to pick out the time of Chaucer, the Elizabethan age, the mid-eighteenth century, possibly the Edwardian age.

[4] I exclude the poorer two-thirds of the world, not because I believe that the conclusions reached about the advantages of sustained economic growth would differ that much for their predicament. But the issues are rather different and the questions we should ask are rather different.

[5] To choose a topical example, do we really need exhaustive psychological tests to determine whether the manifest increase in violence and sadistic cruelty that is depicted on mass media over the last two decades influences people for the worse? Is it not a reflection of the obsession with measurement, which typifies the technological society, that we feel impelled to undertake prolonged experimentation and to employ all the impressive paraphernalia of advanced statistics

in order to discover something which should be obvious to a half-wit—or to put the matter more sedately, to confirm a fact of life that is part of the common psychological experience of the human race since the dawn of civilization?

Why do parents instinctively avert their children's eyes from unexpected scenes of violence? Where has it been proposed that parents should be visibly cruel to one another, on the cathartic hypothesis that in consequence their children would become the gentlest of lovers? When, on the same theory, was a drunk and obscene father regarded as a good influence? Why do we so readily accept the view that the brutal atmosphere of a prison can exert a brutalizing influence on the character of the inmates? And yet we are asked to suspend the judgment of our instincts, our senses, and our experience, and to consider seriously the possibility that scenes of repeated cruelty, scenes of cool and casual violence, scenes of sadistic titillation, seen day after day by the young and impressionable, will have no influence, other than a benign one, on their character or on their ideas of what is normal and acceptable behavior!

The very least that should be said as a guide to action is that since there is and has been, for millennia, a strong presumption that "bad examples" are bad, social policy should be guided by it until evidence to the contrary is overwhelming and irresistible. Our existing policy, in this respect as in many others in a commercial and economic-growth-dominated ethos, is of course the reverse of this.

[6] The standard euphemism is, of course, "highly motivated," a condition that is looked upon not as an aberration but as a virtue.

[7] The theme that economic feasibility is not enough, and has not, in fact, prevailed against vested commercial and political interests, has been developed recently in connection with water pollution in the United States by A. M. Freeman and R. H. Haveman, "Clean Rhetoric, Dirty Water," *The Public Interest* (Summer 1972).

[8] We may want to include the strengthening of the country's defenses and, in the world of today, it might be thought that we can use as much growth as we can get. But the proportion that the United States spends on defense today is well under 10 percent of GNP, and, of the sum which that represents, only a fraction is used in research. Ignoring inefficiency in

the ways funds are spent by the Defense Department, and ignoring costly mistakes of the State Department, the cost of research directed toward maintaining national security and keeping us abreast of the arms race could be continued for a long time without the economy having to grow.

Nor is the "spin-off" contention very convincing. Modern research is increasingly specialized: the bulk of industry's innovation stems from its own research. Defense is no exception.

These remarks are, however, tentative, and I am open to persuasion of the need, in today's uncertain political climate, for particular kinds of research and growth for defense purposes.

[9] If this is what we do mean, we should bear in mind that the aid given to these poor countries by the West is slight. The United States, the chief donor, gives sums that total much less than one-half of one percent of her GNP. And though it is a comfort to believe that while you are munching your cake, the crumbs are not entirely going to waste, charity on this microscopic scale can hardly justify the pursuit of economic growth by the West. We might agree to consider the question afresh if we ever decide to donate a sizable proportion of our incomes to the poor living outside the West.

As for the help these poorer countries might derive from trade with Western countries that continue to grow at postwar rates, this is a controversial issue, especially in view of the Chinese experience, and I shall not discuss it here except to remark that the West would be faced with a moral dilemma if it were agreed that our further economic growth was bad for us but good for them.

[10] See my article in *Daedalus* (Fall 1973).

[11] I am aware that the Clean Air Act of 1957 in Britain did much to reduce the sulfur and carbon dioxide content of the air, and the danger of fogs. The carbon monoxide content has, of course, been steadily increasing. The Thames is today a little cleaner that it was a score of years ago. But these local improvements are slight compared with the spoliation of the countryside and the global pollution about which concern is growing year by year.

[12] See my *Costs of Economic Growth*, Parts I and II.

[13] The connections between increased affluence and crime have not been made explicit. Statistics have been produced to show that crime in the United States is positively related to

city size, and though this may be particular to the United States, there would seem to be a relation between affluence and crime across countries. Certainly crime has been rapidly rising in all Western nations since the war, partly perhaps as a result of the drift to the towns, itself a direct consequence of economic growth (since less agricultural labor is needed), partly, one conjectures, because of the greater opportunities for quick enrichment (in which the fast getaway automobile plays a large part), along with the erosion of moral standards (attributable to the growth in secular knowledge and the growth of porno-violence in mass media entertainment).

14 The melancholia of which Boswell complained was not uncommon in the latter part of the eighteenth century, and has been attributed by some historians to the erosion of religious faith that came in the wake of the Enlightenment. It was to spread further down through the strata of society after Darwin's *Origin of Species*. The anguish of so sensitive a writer as Charlotte Bronte on reading the atheistic arguments of Harriet Martineau and others is sympathetically portrayed in Mrs. Gaskell's biography (Chapter 23).

15 During the war, I did guard duty one night for a friend, who, to show his gratitude, gave me a bar of chocolate the next morning. I still love chocolate, but it was a scarce item during the war, and I was touched by his thoughtfulness. I recall also an American journalist visiting Britain in the spring of 1941 who gave his cabbie a pound of tea as a tip. The cabbie was overjoyed, invited him to his home, and insisted that he should call him any time of the day or night that he wanted a lift.

I could multiply such instances — but not in an affluent society.

16 The American University Community Center offers its students (in 1972/73), among other therapeutic services, the following:

"Encountertype Groups. — These are personal growth groups designed as structured, encounter experiences focusing on themes of trust building, giving and receiving feedback, direct communication, and sensory awareness. They will serve as an introduction . . . for well-functioning persons.

"Interpersonal Skill Building Groups. — In these ten-

session, skill-focused groups, students will be taught to monitor and master anxiety, using . . . improved social skills by learning to be appropriately assertive, and more direct in empathic communication."

Let us refrain from commenting on this pathetic display of jargon which regards the hapless human as a faulty machine, and wonder instead at the condition of the affluent society whose members have reached such a state of perplexity that things such as trust and the interchange of affection — which should be as natural as breathing and sleeping — must be mastered as a technique.

Yet this response is of the essence of the technological process. For where wisdom would propose a retreat from the path of growth, or the surrender of some specific product or technique, the technocrat invariably proposes an "advance" — the search for more technology in order to mend or patch up the damage created by existing technology.

In order for people to have the freedom to drive fast automobiles, we sacrifice the lives of 55,000 people each year in the United States, and we maim for life several times that number. Few take seriously the proposal to abolish this mode of travel. The only admissible issues are better insurance, more (ineffectual) safety gadgets, and improved hospital facilities.

2 | Is the end of the world at hand?

ROBERT M. SOLOW

I WAS HAVING a hard time figuring out how to begin when I came across an excerpt from an interview with my MIT colleague Professor Jay Forrester, who is either the Christopher Columbus or the Dr. Strangelove of this business, depending on how you look at it. Forrester said he would like to see about a hundred people, the most gifted and best qualified in the world, brought together in a team to make a psychosocial analysis of the problem of world equilibrium. He thought it would take about ten years. When he was asked to define the composition of his problem-solving group, Forrester said: "Above all it shouldn't be mostly made up of professors. One would include people who had been successful in their personal careers, whether in politics, business, or anywhere else. We should also need radical philosophers, but we should take care to keep out representatives of the social sciences. Such people always want to go to the bottom of a particular problem. What we want to look at are the problems caused by interactions." I don't know what you call people who believe they can be wrong about everything in particular, but expect to be lucky enough somehow to get it right on the interactions. They may be descendants of the famous merchant Lapidus, who said he lost money on every item he sold, but made it up on the volume. Well, I suppose that as an economist I am a representative of the social sciences; and I'm prepared to play out the role by talking about first principles and trying to say what the Growth vs. No-Growth business is really all about. This is going to involve me in the old academic ploy of saying over and over again what I'm not talking about before I ever actually say what I think I am talking about. But I'm afraid that some of those boring distinctions are part of the price you have to pay for getting it right.

First of all, there are (at least) two separate questions you can ask about the prospects for economic growth. You can ask: Is growth desirable? Or you can ask: Is growth possible? I suppose that if continued economic growth is not possible, it hardly matters whether or not it's desirable. But if it is possible, it's presumably not inevitable, so we can discuss whether we should want it. But they are separate questions, and an answer to one of them is not necessarily an answer to the other. My main business is with the question about the possibility of continued growth; I want to discuss the validity of the negative answer given by the "Doomsday Models" associated with the names of Forrester and Meadows (and MIT!), and to a lesser extent with the group of English scientists who published a manifesto called "A Blueprint for Survival." Dr. Mishan's main concern, on the other hand, was with the desirability of continued economic growth (and, at least by implication, with the desirability of past economic growth). If I spend a few minutes poaching on his territory, it is mainly because that seems like a good way to get some concepts straight, but also just to keep a discussion going.

Sorting out the issues

Arguments about the desirability of economic growth often turn quickly into arguments about the "quality" of modern life. One gets the notion that you favor growth if you are the sort of person whose idea of heaven is to drive 90 miles an hour down a six-lane highway reading billboards, in order to pollute the air over some crowded lake, itself polluted, with the exhaust from twin 100-horsepower outboards, and whose idea of food is Cocoa Krispies. On the other hand, to be against economic growth is to be a Granola-eating, back-packing, transcendental-meditating canoe freak. That may even be a true statistical association, but I will argue that there is no necessary or logical connection between your answer to the growth question and your answer to the quality-of-life question. Suppose there were no issue about economic growth; suppose it were impossible; suppose each man or each woman were equipped to have only two children (one bomb under each wing); suppose we were stuck with the technology we have now and had no concept of invention, or even of increased mechanization through capital investment. We could still argue about the relative merits of cutting timber for building houses or leaving it stand to be enjoyed as forest. Some people would still be willing to breathe carbon monoxide in big cities in return for the excitement of urban life, while others would prefer cleaner air and fewer TV channels. Macy's would still not tell Gimbel's. Admen would still try to tell you that all those beautiful women are actually just looking for somebody who smokes Winchesters, thus managing to insult both men and women at once. Some people would still bring transistor radios to the beach. All or nearly all of the arguments about the quality of life would be just as valid if the question of growth never arose.

I won't go so far as to say there is no connection. In particular, one can argue that if population density were low enough, people would interfere much less with each other, and everyone could find a part of the world and style of civilization that suited him. Then differences of opinion about the quality of life wouldn't matter so much. Even if I grant the truth of that observation, it is still the case that, from here on out, questions about the quality of life are separable from questions about the desirability of growth. If growth stopped, there would be just about as much to complain about; and, as I shall argue later on, one can imagine continued growth with reductions in pollution and congestion and less consumption of sliced white bread.

I suppose it is only fair to admit that if you get very enthusiastic about economic growth you are likely to be attracted to easily quantifiable and measurable things as objects of study, to point at with pride or to view with alarm. You are likely to pay less attention to important, intangible aspects of the standard of living. Although you can't know whether people are happier than they used to be, you can at least determine that they drink more orange juice or take more aspirin. But that's mere weakness of imagination and has nothing to do in principle with the desirability of economic growth, let alone with its possibility.

There is another practical argument that is often made, and although it is important, it sometimes serves as a way of avoiding coming to grips with the real issues. This argument says that economic growth, increasing output per person, is the only way we are likely to achieve a more equitable distribution of income in society. There is a lot of home truth in that. It is inevitably less likely that a middle-class electorate will vote to redistribute part of its own income to the poor than that it will be willing to allocate a slightly larger share of a growing total. Even more pessimistically, I might suggest that even a given relative distribution of income, supposing it cannot be made more equal for political or other reasons, is less unattractive if the absolute standard of living at the bottom is fairly high than it is if the absolute standard at the bottom is very low. From this point of view, even if economic growth doesn't lead to more equity in distribution, it makes the inequity we've got more tolerable. I think it is one of the lessons of history that this is a realistic statement of the prospects.

It is even clearer if one looks, not at the distribution of income within a rich country like the United States, but at the distribution of income between the developed countries of the world and the underdeveloped ones. The rich Western nations have never been able to agree on the principle of allocating as much as one percent of their GNP to aid underdeveloped countries. They are unlikely to be willing to share their wealth on any substantial scale with the poor countries. Even if they were, there are so many more poor people in the world that an equally shared income would be quite low. The *only* prospect of a decent life for Asia, Africa, and Latin America is in more total output.

But I point this out only to warn you that it is not the heart of the question. I think that those who oppose continued growth should in honesty face up to the implications of their position for distributional equity and the prospects of the world's poor. I think that those who favor continued growth on the grounds that only thus can we achieve some real equality ought to be serious about that. If economic growth with equality is a good thing, it doesn't follow that economic growth with a lot of pious talk about equality is a good thing. In principle, we can have growth with or without equity and we can have stagnation with or without equity. An argument about first principles should keep those things separate.

Sacrificing for posterity

Well, then, what *is* the problem of economic growth all about? (I'm giving a definition now, not stating a fact, so all I can say is that I think this way of looking at it contributes to clarity of thought.) Whenever there is a question about what to *do*, the desirability of economic growth turns on the claims of the future against the claims of the present. The pro-growth man is someone who is prepared to sacrifice something useful and desirable right now so that people should be better off in the future; the anti-growth man is someone who thinks that is unnecessary or undesirable. The nature of the sacrifice of present enjoyment for future enjoyment can be almost anything. The classic example is investment: We can use our labor and our resources to build very durable things like roads or subways or factories or blast furnaces or dams that will be used for a long time by people who were not even born when those things were created, and so will certainly have contributed nothing to their construction. That labor and those resources can just as well be used to produce shorter-run pleasures for us now.

Such a sacrifice of current consumption on behalf of the future may not strike you as much of a sacrifice. But that's because you live in a country that is already rich; if you had lived in Stalin's Russia, that need to sacrifice would be one of the reasons you would have been given to explain why you had to live without comfort and pleasures while the Ministry of Heavy Industry got all the play. If you lived in an underdeveloped country now, you would face the same problem: What shall you do with the foreign currency earned by sales of cocoa or copper or crude oil—spend it on imports of consumer goods for those alive and working now, or spend it on imports of machinery to start building an industry that may help to raise the standard of living in thirty years' time?

There are other ways in which the same choice can be made, including, for instance, the direction of intellectual resources to the invention of things (like the generation of electricity from nuclear fusion) that will benefit future generations. Paradoxically, one of the ways in which the present can do something for the future is to conserve natural resources. If we get along with less lumber now so that there will be more forests standing for our grandchildren, or if we limit the present consumption of oil or zinc so that there will be some left for the twenty-first century, or if we worry about siltation behind dams that would otherwise be fun for fishermen and water-skiers, in all those cases we are promoting economic growth. I call that paradoxical because I think most people identify the conservation freak with the anti-growth party whereas, in this view of the matter, the conservationist is trading present satisfaction for future satisfaction, that is, he is promoting economic growth. I think the confusion comes from mixing up the quality-of-life problem with the growth problem. But it is nonetheless a confusion.

Why should we be concerned with the welfare of posterity, given the indubitable fact that posterity has never done a thing for us? I am not anthropologist enough to know how rare or common it is that our culture should teach us to care not only about our children but about their children, and *their* children. I suppose there are good Darwinian reasons why cultures without any future-orientation should fail to survive very long in the course of history. (But remember that they had a merry time of it while they lasted!) Moreover, we now enjoy the investments made by our ancestors, so there is a kind of equity in passing it on. Also, unless something terrible happens, there will be a lot more future

than there has been past; and, for better or worse—
probably worse—there will be more people at each future instant than there are now or have been. So all in
all, the future will involve many more man-years of life
than the present or the past, and a kind of intergenerational democracy suggests that all those man-years-to-be
deserve some consideration out of sheer numbers.

On the other hand, *if* continued economic
growth is possible—which is the question I'm coming
to—then it is very likely that posterity will be richer
than we are even if we make no special efforts on its
behalf. If history offers any guide, then, in the developed part of the world at least, the accumulation of technological knowledge will probably make our great-
grandchildren better off than we are, even if we make
no great effort in that direction. Leaving aside the possibility of greater equality—I have already discussed
that—there is hardly a crying need for posterity to be
on average very much richer than we are. Why should
us poor folk make any sacrifices for those who will in
any case live in luxury in the future? Of course, if the
end of the world is at hand, if continued economic
growth is *not* possible, then we ought to care more about
posterity, because they won't be so well off. Paradoxically, if continued economic growth is not possible, or
less possible, then we probably ought to do more to promote it. Actually, there's no paradox in that, as every
student of economics will realize, because it is a way of
saying that the marginal return on investment is high.

Overshoot and collapse

There is, as you know, a school of thought that
claims that continued economic growth is in fact not
possible any more, or at least not for very long. This

judgment has been expressed more or less casually by several observers in recent years. What distinguishes the Doomsday Models from their predecessors is that they claim to much more than a casual judgment: they deduce their beliefs about future prospects from mathematical models or systems analysis. They don't merely say that the end of the world is at hand—they can show you computer output that says the same thing.

Characteristically, the Doomsday Models do more than just say that continued economic growth is impossible. They tell us why: in brief, because (a) the earth's natural resources will soon be used up; (b) increased industrial production will soon strangle us in pollution; and (c) increasing population will eventually outrun the world's capacity to grow food, so that famine must eventually result. And, finally, the models tell us one more thing: the world will end with a bang, not a whimper. The natural evolution of the world economy is not at all toward some kind of smooth approach to its natural limits, wherever they are. Instead, it is inevitable—unless we make drastic changes in the way we live and organize ourselves—that the world will overshoot any level of population and production it can possibly sustain and will then collapse, probably by the middle of the next century.

I would like to say why I think that the Doomsday Models are bad science and therefore bad guides to public policy. I hope nobody will conclude that I believe the problems of population control, environmental degradation, and resource exhaustion to be unimportant, or that I am one of those people who believe that an adequate response to such problems is a vague confidence that some technological solution will turn up. On the contrary, it is precisely because these are important problems that public policy had better be based on sound and careful analysis. I want to explain some of my reasons for believing that the global models don't provide even the beginnings of a foundation of that kind.

The first thing to realize is that the characteristic conclusion of the Doomsday Models is very near the surface. It is, in fact, more nearly an assumption than a conclusion, in the sense that the chain of logic from the assumptions to the conclusion is very short and rather obvious.

The basic assumption is that stocks of things like the world's natural resources and the waste-disposal capacity of the environment are finite, that the world economy tends to consume the stock at an increasing rate (through the mining of minerals and the production of goods), and that there are no built-in mechanisms by which approaching exhaustion tends to turn off consumption gradually and in advance. You hardly need a giant computer to tell you that a system with those behavior rules is going to bounce off its ceiling and collapse to a low level. Then, in case anyone is inclined to relax into the optimistic belief that maybe things aren't that bad, we are told: Imagine that the stock of natural resources were actually twice as big as the best current evidence suggests, or imagine that the annual amount of pollution could be halved all at once and then set to growing again. All that would happen is that the date of collapse would be postponed by T years, where T is not a large number. But once you grasp the quite simple essence of the models, this should come as no surprise. It is important to realize where these powerful conclusions come from, because, if you ask yourself "Why didn't I realize earlier that the end of the world was at hand?" the answer is not that you weren't clever enough to figure it out for yourself. The answer is that the imminent end of the world is an immediate deduction from certain assumptions, and one must really ask if the assumptions are any good.

It is a commonplace that if you calculate the annual output of any production process, large or small, and divide it by the annual employment of labor, you get a ratio that is called the productivity of labor. At the most aggregative level, for example, we can say that the GNP in 1971 was $1,050 billion and that about 82 million people were employed in producing it, so that GNP per worker or the productivity of a year of labor was about $12,800. Symmetrically, though the usage is less common, one could just as well calculate the GNP per unit of some particular natural resource and call that the productivity of coal, or GNP per pound of vanadium. We usually think of the productivity of labor as rising more or less exponentially, say at 2 or 3 percent a year, because that is the way it has in fact behaved over the past century or so since the statistics began to be collected. The rate of increase in the productivity of labor is not a constant of nature. Sometimes it is faster, sometimes slower. For example, we know that labor productivity must have increased more slowly a long time ago, because if we extrapolate backward at 2 percent a year, we come to a much lower labor productivity in 1492 than can possibly have been the case. And the productivity of labor has risen faster in the past twenty-five years than in the fifty years before that. It also varies from place to place, being faster in Japan and Germany and slower in Great Britain, for reasons that are not at all certain. But it rises, and we expect it to keep rising.

Now, how about the productivity of natural resources? All the Doomsday Models will allow is a one-time hypothetical increase in the world supply of natural resources, which is the equivalent of a one-time increase in the productivity of natural resources. Why shouldn't the productivity of most natural resources rise more or less steadily through time, like the productivity of labor? And of course it does for some resources, but not for others. Real GNP roughly doubled between 1950 and 1970. But the consumption of primary and scrap iron increased by about 20 percent, so the productivity of iron, GNP per ton of iron, increased by about 2.5 percent a year on the average during those twenty years. The U. S. consumption of manganese rose by 30 percent in the same period, so the productivity of manganese went up by some 70 percent in twenty years, a bit under 2.25 percent a year. Aggregate consumption of nickel just about doubled, like GNP, so the productivity of nickel didn't change. U. S. consumption of copper, both primary and secondary, went up by a third between 1951 and 1970, so GNP per pound of copper rose at 2 percent a year on the average. The story on lead and zinc is very similar, so their productivity increased at some 2 percent a year. The productivity of bituminous coal rose at 3 percent a year.

Naturally, there are important exceptions, and unimportant exceptions. GNP per barrel of oil was about the same in 1970 as in 1951: no productivity increase there. The consumption of natural gas tripled in the same period, so GNP per cubic foot of natural gas fell at about 2.5 percent a year. Our industrial demand for aluminum quadrupled in two decades, so that productivity of aluminum fell at a good 3.5 percent a year. And industrial demand for columbium was multiplied by a factor of 25: in 1951 we managed $2.25 million of GNP (in 1967 prices) per pound of columbium, whereas in 1970 we were down to $170,000 of GNP per pound of columbium. On the other hand, it is a little hard to imagine civilization toppling because of a shortage of columbium.

Obviously, many forces combine to govern the course of the productivity of any given mineral over time. When a rare natural resource is first available, it acquires new uses with a rush; and consumption goes up much faster than GNP. That's the columbium story, no doubt, and, to a lesser extent, the vanadium story. But once the novelty has worn off, the productivity of a resource tends to rise as better or worse substitutes for it appear, as new commodities replace old ones, and as manufacturing processes improve. One of the reasons the productivity of copper rises is because that of aluminum falls, as aluminum replaces copper in many uses. The same is true of coal and oil. A resource like petroleum, which is versatile because of its role as a source of energy, is an interesting special case. It is hardly any wonder that the productivity of petroleum has stagnated, since the consumption of energy—both as electricity for domestic and industrial use and in the automobile—has recently increased even faster than GNP. But no one can doubt that we will run out of oil, that coal and nuclear fission will replace oil as the major sources of energy. It is already becoming probable that the high-value use of oil will soon be as feed stock for the petrochemical industries, rather than as a source of energy. Sooner or later, the productivity of oil will rise out of sight, because the production and consumption of oil will eventually dwindle toward zero, but real GNP will not.

So there really is no reason why we should not think of the productivity of natural resources as increasing more or less exponentially over time. But then overshoot and collapse are no longer the inevitable trajectory of the world system, and the typical assumption-conclusion of the Doomsday Models falls by the wayside. We are in a different sort of ball game. The system might still burn itself out and collapse in finite time, but one cannot say with any honesty that it must. It all depends on the particular, detailed facts of modern economic life as well as on the economic policies that we and the rest of the world pursue. I don't want to argue for any particular counterstory; all I want to say now is that the overshoot-collapse pattern is built into the models very near the surface, by assumption, and by implausible assumption at that.

Scarcity and the price system

There is at least one reason for believing that the Doomsday story is almost certainly wrong. The most glaring defect of the Forrester-Meadows models is the absence of any sort of functioning price system. I am no believer that the market is always right, and I am certainly no advocate of *laissez-faire* where the environment is concerned. But the price system is, after all, the main social institution evolved by capitalist economies (and, to an increasing extent, socialist economies too) for registering and reacting to relative scarcity. There are several ways in which the working of the price system will push our society into faster and more systematic increases in the productivity of natural resources.

First of all, let me go back to the analogy between natural resources and labor. We are not surprised to learn that industry quite consciously tries to make inventions that save labor, i.e., permit the same product to be made with fewer man-hours of work. After all, on the average, labor costs amount to almost three-fourths of all costs in our economy. An invention that reduces labor requirements per unit of GNP by 1 percent reduces all costs by about 0.75 percent. Natural resource costs are a much smaller proportion of total GNP, something nearer 5 percent. So industry and engineering have a much stronger motive to reduce labor requirements by 1 percent than to reduce resource requirements by 1 percent, assuming—which may or may not be true—that it is about as hard to do one as to do the other. But then, as the earth's supply of particular natural resources nears exhaustion, and as natural resources become more and more valuable, the motive to economize those natural resources should become as strong as the motive to economize labor. The productivity of resources should rise faster than now—it is hard to imagine otherwise.

There are other ways in which the market mechanism can be expected to push us all to economize on natural resources as they become scarcer. Higher and rising prices of exhaustible resources lead competing producers to substitute other materials that are more plentiful and therefore cheaper. To the extent that it is impossible to design around or find substitutes for expensive natural resources, the prices of commodities that contain a lot of them will rise relative to the prices of other goods and services that don't use up a lot of resources. Consumers will be driven to buy fewer resource-intensive goods and more of other things. All these effects work automatically to increase the productivity of natural resources, i.e., to reduce resource requirements per unit of GNP.

As I mentioned a moment ago, this is not an argument for *laissez-faire*. We may feel that the private decisions of buyers and sellers give inadequate representation to future generations. Or we may feel that private interests are in conflict with a distinct public interest—strip-mining of coal is an obvious case in point, and there are many others as soon as we begin to think about environmental effects. Private market responses may be too uncoordinated, too slow, based on insufficient and faulty information. In every case there will be actions that public agencies can take and should take; and it will be a major political struggle to see that they are taken. But I don't see how one can have the slightest confidence in the predictions of models that seem to make no room for the operation of everyday market forces. If the forecasts are wrong, then so are the policy implications, to the extent that there are any realistic policy implications.

Every analysis of resource scarcity has to come to terms with the fact that the prices of natural resources and resource products have not shown any tendency to rise over the past half century, relative to the prices of other things. This must mean that there have so far been adequate offsets to any progressive impoverishment of deposits—like improvements in the technology of extraction, savings in end uses, or the availability of cheaper substitutes. The situation could, of course, change; and very likely some day it will. If the experienced and expert participants in the market now believed that resource prices would be sharply higher at some foreseeable time, prices would *already* be rising, as I will try to explain in a moment. The historical steadiness of resource prices suggests that buyers and sellers in the market have not been acting as if they foresaw exhaustion in the absence of substitutes, and therefore sharply higher future prices. They may turn out to be wrong; but the Doomsday Models give us absolutely no reason to expect that—in fact, they claim to get whatever meager empirical basis they have from such experts.

Why is it true that if the market saw higher prices in the future, prices would already be rising? It is a rather technical point, but I want to explain it because, in a way, it summarizes the important thing about natural resources: conserving a mineral deposit is just as much of an investment as building a factory, and it has to be analyzed that way. Any owner of a mineral deposit owns a valuable asset, whether the owner is a private capitalist or the government of an underdeveloped country. The asset is worth keeping only if at the margin it earns a return equal to that earned on other kinds of assets. A factory produces things each year of its life, but a mineral deposit just lies there: its owner can realize a return only if he either mines the deposit or if it *increases in value.* So if you are sitting on your little pile of X and confidently expect to be able to sell it for a very high price in the year 2000 because it will be very scarce by then, you must be earning your 5 percent a year, or 10 percent a year, or whatever the going rate of return is, each year between now and 2000. The only way this can happen is for the value of X to go up by 5 percent a year or 10 percent a year. And that means that anyone who wants to use any X any time between now and 2000 will have to pay a price for it that is rising at that same 5 percent or 10 percent a year. Well, it's not happening. Of course we are exploiting our hoard of exhaustible resources; we have no choice about that. We are certainly exploiting it wastefully, in the sense that we allow each other to dump waste products into the environment without full accounting for costs. But there is very little evidence that we are exploiting it too fast.

Population growth

I have less to say about the question of population growth because it does not seem to involve any difficult conceptual problems. At any time, in any place, there is presumably an optimal size of population—with the property that the average person would be somewhat worse off if the population were a bit larger, and also worse off if the population were a bit smaller. In any real case it must be very difficult to know what the optimum population is, especially because it will change over time as technology changes, and also because it is probably more like a band or zone than a sharply defined number. I mean that if you could somehow plot a graph of economic welfare per person against population size, there would be a very gentle dome or plateau at the top, rather than a sharp peak.

I don't intend to guess what the optimal population for the United States may be. But I am prepared to hazard the guess that there is no point in opting for a perceptibly larger population than we now have, and we might well be content with a slightly smaller one. (I want to emphasize the likelihood that a 15 percent larger or 15 percent smaller population would make very little difference in our standard of well-being. I also want to emphasize that I am talking only about our own country. The underdeveloped world offers very special problems.) My general reason for believing that we should not want a substantially larger population is this. We all know the bad consequences of too large a population: crowding, congestion, excessive pollution, the disappearance of open space—that is why the curve of average well-being eventually turns down at large population sizes. Why does the curve ever climb to a peak in the first place? The generic reason is what economists call economies of scale, because it takes a population of a certain size and density to support an efficient chemical industry, or publishing industry, or symphony orchestra, or engineering university, or airline, or computer hardware and software industry, especially if you would like several firms in each, so that they can be partially regulated by their own competition. But after all, it only takes a population of a *certain* size or density to get the benefit of these economies of scale. And I'm prepared to guess that the U. S. economy is already big enough to do so; I find it hard to believe that sheer efficiency would be much served in the United States by having a larger market.

As it happens, recent figures seem to show that the United States is heading for a stationary population: that is to say, the current generation of parents seems to be establishing fertility patterns that will, if continued, cause the population to stabilize some time during the next century. Even so, the absolute size of the population will increase for a while, and level off higher than it is now, because decades of population growth have left us with a bulge of population in the childbearing ages. But I have already argued that a few million more or less hardly make a difference; and a population that has once stabilized might actually decrease, if that came to seem desirable.

At the present moment, at least for the United States, the danger of rapid population growth seems to be the wrong thing to worry about. The main object of public policy in this field ought to be to ensure that the choice of family size is truly a voluntary choice, that access to the best birth-control methods be made universal. That seems to be all that is needed. Of course, we know very little about what governs fertility, about why the typical notion of a good family size changes from generation to generation. So it is certainly possible that these recent developments will reverse themselves and that population control will again appear on the agenda of public policy. This remains to be seen.

In all this I have said nothing about the Doomsday Models because there is practically nothing that needs to be said. So far as we can tell, they make one very bad mistake: in the face of reason, common sense, and systematic evidence they seem to assume that at high standards of living, people want more children as they become more affluent (though over most of the observed range, a higher standard of living goes along with smaller families). That is certainly a bad error in terms of the recent American data—but perhaps it explains why some friends of mine were able to report that they had run a version of the Forrester World Dynamic Model starting with a population of two people and discovered that it blew up in 500 years. Apart from placing the date of the Garden of Eden in the fifteenth century, what else is new?

There is another analytical error in the models, as Fred Singer has pointed out. Suppose resource exhaustion and increased pollution conspire to bring about a reduction in industrial production. The model then says that birth rates will rise because, in the past, low industrial output has been associated with high birth rates. But there is nothing in historical evidence to suggest that a once-rich country will go *back* to high birth rates if (as I doubt will happen) its standard of living falls from an accustomed high level. Common sense suggests that a society in such a position would fight to preserve its standard of living by reducing the desired family size. In any case, this is another example of a poorly founded—or unfounded—assumption introduced to support the likelihood of overshoot-and-collapse.

Paying for pollution

Resource exhaustion and overpopulation: that leaves pollution as the last of the Doomsday Devils. The subject is worth a whole lecture in itself, because it is one of those problems about which economists actually have something important to say to the world, not just to each other. But I must be brief. Fine print aside, I think that what one gets from the Doomsday literature is the notion that air and water and noise pollution are an inescapable accompaniment of economic growth, especially industrial growth. If that is true, then to be against pollution is to be against growth. I realize that in putting the matter so crudely I have been unjust; nevertheless, that is the message that comes across. I think that way of looking at the pollution problem is wrong.

A correct analysis goes something like this. Excessive pollution and degradation of the environment certainly accompany industrial growth and the increasing population density that goes with it. But they are by no means an inescapable by-product. Excessive pollution occurs because of an important flaw in the price system. Factories, power plants, municipal sewers, drivers of cars, strip-miners of coal and deep-miners of coal, and all sorts of generators of waste are allowed to dump that waste into the environment, into the atmosphere and into running water and the oceans, without paying the full cost of what they do. No wonder they do too much. So would you, and so would I. In fact, we actually do—directly as drivers of cars, indirectly as we buy some products at a price which is lower than it ought to be because the producer is not required to pay for using the environment to carry away his wastes, and even more indirectly as we buy things that are made with things that pollute the environment.

This flaw in the price system exists because a scarce resource (the waste-disposal capacity of the environment) goes unpriced; and that happens because it is owned by all of us, as it should be. The flaw can be corrected, either by the simple expedient of regulating the discharge of wastes to the environment by direct control or by the slightly more complicated device of charging special prices—user taxes—to those who dispose of wastes in air or water. These effluent charges do three things: they make pollution-intensive goods expensive, and so reduce the consumption of them; they make pollution-intensive methods of production costly, and so promote abatement of pollution by producers; they generate revenue that can, if desired, be used for the further purification of air or water or for other en-

vironmental improvements. Most economists prefer this
device of effluent charges to regulation by direct order.
This is more than an occupational peculiarity. Use of the
price system has certain advantages in efficiency and
decentralization. Imposing a physical limit on, say, sulfur dioxide emission is, after all, a little peculiar. It says
that you may do so much of a bad thing and pay nothing
for the privilege, but after that, the price is infinite. Not
surprisingly, one can find a more efficient schedule of
pollution abatement through a more sensitive tax schedule.

But this difference of opinion is minor compared with the larger point that needs to be made. The
annual cost that would be necessary to meet decent pollution-abatement standards by the end of the century
is large, but not staggering. One estimate says that in
1970 we spent about $8.5 billion (in 1967 prices), or 1
percent of GNP, for pollution abatement. An active pollution-abatement policy would cost perhaps $50 billion
a year by 2000, which would be about 2 percent of GNP
by then. That is a small investment of resources: you
can see how small it is when you consider that GNP
grows by 4 percent or so every year, on the average.
Cleaning up air and water would entail a cost that would
be a bit like losing one-half of one year's growth between now and the year 2000. What stands between us
and a decent environment is not the curse of industrialization, not an unbearable burden of cost, but just the
need to organize ourselves consciously to do some simple
and knowable things. Compared with the possibility of
an active abatement policy, the policy of stopping economic growth in order to stop pollution would be incred-
ibly inefficient. It would not actually accomplish much,
because one really wants to reduce the amount of, say,
hydrocarbon emission to a third or a half of *what it is
now.* And what no-growth would accomplish, it would

do by cutting off your face to spite your nose.

In the end, that is really my complaint about the Doomsday school. It diverts attention from the really important things that can actually be done, step by step, to make things better. The end of the world *is* at hand—the earth, if you take the long view, will fall into the sun in a few billion years anyway, unless some other disaster happens first. In the meantime, I think we'd be better off trying to pass a strong sulfur-emissions tax, or getting some Highway Trust Fund money allocated to mass transit, or building a humane and decent floor under family incomes, or overriding President Nixon's veto of a strong Water Quality Act, or reforming the tax system, or fending off starvation in Bengal —instead of worrying about the generalized "predicament of mankind."

3 | Can technological progress continue to provide for the future?

MELVIN KRANZBERG

As AN HISTORIAN, I am obligated to point out that technology did not progress very rapidly for most of man's history. Until the last two centuries, technology developed irregularly and at so slow a pace that, for most of human history, the mass of mankind lived in a world of scarcity and deprivation. The Industrial Revolution ushered in an era of rapid technological advance. In accelerating measure since then, technological developments have increased man's control over his environment, ministered to his animal needs and creature comforts, rescued him from the ever-present fear of starvation, increased his mobility, lengthened his lifespan, and, in general, made work easier and life more comfortable for most of the population in the industrialized nations of the world.

Man's technical progress in the nineteenth century was dramatic; in the first seven decades of the twentieth century it has been spectacular. At the beginning of the nineteenth century, men could travel only as fast as a horse or sailing vessel could carry them, and these speeds had not increased significantly across the centuries. By 1900 the railroad was moving men across land at speeds up to 70 miles an hour, and steamships moved faster and more surely than the swiftest of clipper ships. In 1800 a man's voice could be heard only by those within shouting distance; by 1900 the telegraph and telephone were carrying the human voice across continents. In 1800, when a man died, his voice and actions were buried with him; in 1900 the phonograph and the newly invented motion-picture machine recorded him for posterity. In 1800 most Americans went to bed at dusk or perhaps stayed up a few hours later to read by the light of the fireplace or of flickering candles; by 1900 sundown did not mean bedtime, for there were gaslights, newfangled electric lights and, in the remote countryside, kerosene lamps to illumine the darkness. The progress of mechanization in the nineteenth century had relieved man from many backbreaking tasks on the farm and in the factories, and had enormously increased the output of manufactured goods.

Given this record of past performance, it is not surprising that men in the year 1900 looked back with satisfaction over what had been accomplished during the preceding century and looked forward with blithe confidence and naive hope that technology would do still more for them in the century to come. Bearing a faith which might be termed "industrial humanism," they expected that the technological revolution in production and distribution would bring a brave new world into being. Poverty would be abolished; technology's benefits would spread worldwide to do away with misery and insecurity and hence with class and international warfare.

Well, a funny thing happened on the way to Utopia. Here we are three-quarters of the way through the twentieth century, and the promises of social betterment, world peace, and material progress have not yet materialized. But we cannot blame technology for all that went wrong. Indeed, technology more than made good on its promises of quickened transportation and communication, of new sources of energy, and of more material goods and comforts.

But the social promise held forth by an advancing technology did not materialize. I think that is largely because we utilized our technology in the context of an old economy of scarcity, with values and institutions which had been made obsolete by scientific and technological developments. Social benefits were achieved, to be sure, but not to the extent possible if we had renovated our institutions and values by social innovations to accompany, and perhaps point the way for, our technological prowess.

Technology can provide for the future

In light of our recent record, can technological progress continue to provide for the future? My answer to this question is yes. Technological advance can, will, and must provide for the future economic growth which is necessary to meet the needs and wants of our American society and of people throughout the world. But, as we shall see, this technological advance must be guided by social controls which will enable us to employ our technology more effectively. These social controls will arise from new institutions, new values, and new mechanisms which now exist in embryonic form.

Not everyone would agree with my optimistic view regarding future growth. At the very beginning of this year thirty-three distinguished British scientists published "A Blueprint for Survival" in *The Ecologist,* in which they warned that an ecological breakdown was imminent unless population growth, the demand on resources, and economic growth were brought to a quick halt. Although concentrating on the British situation, the blueprint was directed at worldwide problems, and it was a thoroughgoing indictment of current technological and social trends which, it was claimed, were leading the world to the brink of environmental disaster.

Only a month later the British scientific doomsayers were reinforced in their prophecies by an international group of systems analysts based at MIT. The MIT study of world trends concluded that society probably faces an uncontrollable and disastrous collapse within a hundred years unless it moves quickly to establish a "global equilibrium" in which growth of population and industrial output is halted. Peering into the future by building a mathematical model of the world system, this study examined the highly complex interrelations among populations, food supply, natural resources, pollution, and industrial production. *The Limits to Growth,* as the preliminary study is called, argues that the limits to human population in relation to our planet's finite resources are very near, and that the day of doom is virtually upon us.

The MIT study, which forms part of the Club of Rome's "Project on the Predicament of Mankind"—a study whose title almost dictates what the results will be—concludes that if we let things go on as they have been, there will be a precipitous drop in population before the year 2100, presumably through disease and starvation, and the complete breakdown of our industrial society.

Frightened and impressed as I am by the predictions of my colleagues engaged in this game of systems analysis, I still remain an historian. Hence I tend to view all such predictions and projections in the light of historical perspective.

Let us remember what Ralph Waldo Emerson said in his famous Phi Beta Kappa speech at Harvard more than a century ago, when he gave this advice to the American scholar in times of crisis: "Let him not quit his belief that a popgun is a popgun, though the ancient and the honorable of the earth affirm it to be the crack of doom."

In trying to determine whether this is merely the snap of a popgun or a crack of doom, I have the feeling that we have heard the same arguments before. I derive solace from the fact that people have been crying "Wolf!" for many years, and the wolf did not arrive on the scene. Almost two centuries ago, Thomas Robert Malthus theorized that population grew geometrically while food supply grew arithmetically, so that population would soon outstrip available food supply. Malthus proved to be wrong because he did not foresee the Industrial Revolution which was just getting started in Britain at that time and the concomitant transformation in agricultural production.

In the twentieth century the neo-Malthusians arose once again to challenge the ability of technological advancement to meet the material needs of the world's population. Only half a dozen years ago there were dire predictions of global starvation because of the apparent inability to increase agricultural production in relation to the exploding populations. A headline of November 6, 1966 in *The New York Times* read as follows: "Half the World Is Hungry, and Worse Is to Come," and the article, by no less an authority than Drew Middleton, usually a calm and judicious correspondent, predicted that 1985 might well see "man's greatest crisis, a crisis arising out of his failure to perform an elementary task—feeding himself." A book published by William and Paul Paddock in the following year (1967) was entitled *Famine —1975! America's Decision: Who Will Survive?* The grim solution offered by the Paddock brothers ran along desperate lines: the developed nations would have to establish a rank order list of priorities among the hungry nations to decide which should be given food and technical help to become self-sufficient countries; the rest were to be abandoned to starvation. In effect, their solution was to have the industrially advanced nations determine which people of the world would survive.

But the neo-Malthusians were again confounded. A great transformation, the Green Revolution, by introducing recently developed high-yield varieties of rice and wheat, offered new hope to developing nations. New strains of rice and wheat were introduced in the mid-1960s, and by the end of 1966 a production explosion had occurred in the grain bowls of the world. The Philippines, which had imported one million tons of rice annually, became self-sufficient; by 1970, India's wheat production had risen 50 percent, and Ceylon's rice crop had increased 34 percent. In Mexico, wheat yields, which averaged about 500 pounds per acre in 1950, advanced to 2,300. Japan, long an importer of rice, produced a huge surplus.

Such evidence does not make the purveyors of doom change their minds; it merely makes them change their arguments. While grudgingly admitting that the specter of mass starvation has been averted, at least temporarily, the doomsayers point to the harmful ecological side effects of the Green Revolution. Growing the new rice and wheat crops requires large amounts of fertilizer and pesticides, with consequent environmental pollution on a massive scale. We have merely exchanged the immediate problem of mass starvation, they say, for the long-range problem of death to humans and other living creatures by destruction of the environment.

Despite the familiarity of their gloomy prophecies, we cannot dismiss lightly the warnings of the Club of Rome. Just because the Malthusians and neo-Malthusians proved wrong in the past does not mean that they might not be correct now in their forebodings. If we compare them to the boy in the fable who cried "Wolf!" we must remember that, at the end of that story, the wolf finally did come and made a clean sweep of the lambs. In other words, this might not be another false alarm; this might be the real thing.

Meadows and his associates claim that it *is* the real thing, and they proclaim a sense of urgency. The reason for their concern stems, I think, from the fact that they are experts in the computer sciences; hence they understand the implications of exponential growth. They recognize how, as population and per capita consumption grow, the demand curve suddenly zooms upward.

I can share their concern about the finitude of our planet's resources in relation to continued growth, but I cannot share their alarm. From the perspective of history, I can see no cases where exponential growth continued to such extremes that the entire system broke down.

The uses of statistics

I am not opposed to the employment of statistical data in historical interpretation; I applaud its use, especially in a systems analysis which recognizes the interrelatedness of many different factors with the feedbacks operating among them. In brief, I am greatly in favor of the systems-analysis methodology used by the study group of the Club of Rome, and I hope that it can be extended and refined to increase our understanding of yesterday, today, and tomorrow. Nevertheless, as an historian concerned with the complex murkiness of human affairs, I find some major omissions and deficiencies in their systems diagnosis and their no-growth prescription.

One obvious deficiency in an analysis which relies wholly upon statistics is the fact that we don't have sufficient data about enough things to give us a complete picture of what is happening in the world. Life and society occur in a four-dimensional continuum, whereas statistics provide us only with a partial, two-dimensional picture of human activities. Economists sometimes become so enamored with numbers that they disregard the facts behind the figures and hence are blind to the social components of the economic changes which they believe they are measuring.

John Clapham, the great economic historian, skillfully employed production figures in analyzing the economic growth of Western Europe during the nineteenth century. Bedazzled—and perhaps misled—by his carefully constructed statistical syntheses, Clapham achieved the tour de force of writing a two-volume economic history of France and Britain during the nineteenth century without even mentioning the term "Industrial Revolution."

Clapham's myopic view of industrialization still persists. In a recent seminar discussion I happened to mention the phrase "Industrial Revolution." One of academia's most respected statistical economists chided me for using the term, pointing out that production figures for Britain in the century 1760-1860 rose only a few percentage points; this, he said, could scarcely be considered revolutionary. I am certain that his statistics were correct, but I am equally convinced that his conclusion was faulty. For the fact remains that in 1760 the great bulk of Englishmen lived and worked as had their ancestors for thousands of years previously; the hearth and home were the centers of production, and men lived in small rural communities with agriculture as their chief occupation. A hundred years later men had been wrenched from traditional modes of working and living: the factory had become the center of production, and men were dwelling in urban industrial towns, not in rural agrarian villages. By almost every social and cultural index one might employ, the old way of life had been destroyed, and new values, institutions, and attitudes had come into being. I call that a revolution, and I call it an Industrial Revolution because technological developments had brought about the industrialization of Britain and had wrought this great transformation in society and culture. By concentrating on only one set of economic indicators, our great academic statistician had lost sight of other factors which would have given him a truer view of what had actually occurred. Similarly, Robert Fogel, in his econometric analysis of the impact of railroads on American history, comes to the conclusion that they had very little effect—thereby ignoring their profound social and cultural and psychological impact, as well as their effect on other industries and technologies.

My complaint against the MIT group is not that they used statistics incorrectly but that they were unhistorical—although they employed data going back to 1900 in making up their statistical charts—and hence their systems analysis omitted many parameters of the socioeconomic impact of technological developments, as revealed by the history of technology.

Many of the elements which go into making up the technological dynamics of our industrial society cannot be quantified—or at least we have not yet found the way to measure them statistically. These include such things as changing value patterns which modify man's technical choices; his technological creativity, which will undoubtedly enable him to overcome the obstacles to growth; and the development of institutions for social control of technology that will allow us to avert breakdown and still have economic growth, a higher standard of living, and a cleaner environment, and that will improve the quality of life for all the world's inhabitants for the foreseeable future. Let me be more specific.

First, the story of technology, beginning with the age of industrialism, convinces me that the no-growth formula ignores the historical evidence of man's technical creativity. Meadows claims that a rise in industrial capacity, necessitated by a larger world population demanding more goods, will bring about an exhaustion of natural resources; this will in turn force prices up, thereby leaving less money for reinvestment in the capital goods necessary to sustain our industrial base. The history of technology during the last two centuries, however, is the story of an expanding natural-resource base as industrial capacity expanded. Two hundred years ago petroleum played no part among productive resources, and fifty years ago uranium was a mineral of interest only to a few laboratory scientists; but changing technology made both essential for new forms of energy. Twenty years ago the iron mines of the Upper Peninsula in Michigan and the Mesabi Range in Minnesota were considered played out; yet the development of processes for making taconite pellets economically has given them a new lease on life and created natural resources out of what were once considered useless mine tailings.

Of course, the Meadows group will tell us that there is only a finite amount of petroleum resources and iron ore in the earth, and, despite recycling, it will not be sufficient to meet man's growing needs. But this ignores the technologists' demonstrated capability for expanding the resource base and for finding substitutes. Indeed, a material which is coming increasingly into use in this connection is one of man's oldest materials: wood, which is both recyclable and a renewable natural resource.

I am also troubled by the fact that Meadows treats industrial production as a monolithic unit and technology as static. But the industrial base can alter its components, and technology is a dynamic variable which might increase production without strain on resources and without increasing pollution, and at the same time meet the growing demands of a growing population.

The gloomy predictions of the Meadows analysis are produced by extrapolating the present rate of consumption of resources by our present industrial system. But suppose the industrial base alters as a result of technological advances making certain resources cheaper, developing processes for utilization of materials not now considered resources—and suppose all of this is done without any appreciable increase in pollution. We are in the process of doing that right now, and Meadows oversimplifies our industrial system by thinking of it in unitary fashion without recognizing that certain elements can be expanded at greater than the predicted rate without the dire results he predicts.

Let me cite an example of how the complex nature of our industrial system tends to blur the impact of singular developments, revolutionary though they might be in one particular field, and how, therefore, Meadows' simplified analysis can lead us astray. Some half dozen years ago, President Johnson set up a National Commission on Technology, Automation, and Economic Progress. There were dire pronouncements at the time that automation was eliminating 40,000 jobs a week, or 2 million jobs a year, and that this situation would prevail for years to come. There was solid evidence for this view: a recently introduced machine performed 500 manufacturing functions that formerly took 70 men to perform, and in another industrial installation, 48 men with automated equipment replaced 400 men and turned out the same number of finished products in half the time. There is no doubt that computers produce startling gains in productivity when hitched to machines, and they do displace most of the workers formerly employed in those tasks. But the predictions about large-scale unemployment did not materialize. These predictions were based on statistics, but the statistics measured the wrong thing at the wrong time. The introduction of computer-operated devices in manufacturing processes was just beginning to gather momentum; the unemployment extrapolations were made on too small a base, and the impact of computers on employment was blunted by the boom in other sectors of the economy. The fact is that it would have been impossible to separate the computer's effects from those of other elements of accelerating industrialization going on at the same time.

Meadows, I think, makes his mistake in the opposite direction; *he fails to see how improved technical means in certain sectors of industry can alter the very feedback systems upon which he relies so greatly.* The Club of Rome study assumes that advancing industrial production necessarily results in greater pollution. This is simply not true. Newer machines and more sophisticated processes—a result of technological advance and, partially, of public pressure against pollution—actually pollute less and produce more than do the older means. When the Environmental Quality Control Act went into force, many industrialists complained that they would be forced out of business by strict enforcement of pollution standards or that the prices of their products would be so high that they could no longer compete effectively. It has not turned out that way, which demonstrates the ingenuity of our corporate managers as well as of our engineers. True, some factories have had to close; but if the reports are correct, these were older plants which could no longer compete effectively. They have been replaced by new plants which can produce more efficiently and with less pollution. The point is that we are already making inroads against pollution while at the same time increasing production. And if prices have gone up, it is not because our resources are being depleted, as Meadows postulated, but because of inflationary pressures which have little to do with our technological base.

Despite growing industrial production, we are making headway against pollution. For example, England has been so successful in its fight against pollution that certain fish and birds which had not been seen in the Thames River since the early part of the nineteenth century have reappeared. The air in certain American cities is getting cleaner—even in New York City. We are also learning that while Lake Erie might be dying, she is still not dead, and there are high hopes of scouring it out and making it fresh and clean again within the next two decades. In other words, some effects of pollution are not so irreversible as we once thought, as we gain more scientific knowledge and technical expertise.

Indeed, it is possible to make a strong case counter to the Meadows argument. That is, industrial growth rather than industrial no-growth is essential if we are to have sufficient natural resources in the future, if we are to do away with the pollution created by the present state of society, and if we are to take care of the physical needs and creature comforts of the world's growing population. In other words, if my historical analysis could be fed into a computer, it would lead to conclusions exactly the opposite of Meadows'. The population-resource-pollution crises—which he claims can only be resolved by a stabilization of industrial capacity and a sharp reduction in resource consumption—would actually lead me to the opposite conclusion, namely, that we must, by improved scientific technology, develop our resource base and promote our industrial capacity as never before.

The energy factor

But I digress. Let us return again to our critique of the Meadows analysis. It seems inconceivable to me that any attempt to deal with problems involving population growth, pollution, natural resources, industrial output, and food supply should not have considered energy as one of the major parameters in the systems under consideration. Yet I think that the MIT study dismissed energy in a most cavalier fashion.

At the turn of the century the great American historian Henry Adams, fascinated by recent developments in the field of physics, attempted to apply the second law of thermodynamics to human affairs. Using this false analogy, he came to the conclusion that civilization would ultimately break down, for our energy resources—which he also considered finite and irreplaceable—would be dissipated. He thought that our industrial society would founder about the middle of the twentieth century. Well, here we are well on our way in the third quarter of the century, and we are still going strong. Instead of having less energy at our disposal than before, we have an almost unlimited amount available through our capability of exploiting the energy within the atom.

There is no doubt that we will require more energy as we deplete some of the natural resources used in our current technology, and as we recycle in order to extend our present resource base. But with exploitation of nuclear energy we have an almost infinite amount of energy for those purposes and also for converting currently unusable resources into our future resource base.

The entire predictive core of the Meadows systems analysis founders on the fact that it has virtually, though not completely, ignored the essential element in the population-resource-pollution-industrial-food supply equation, namely, the energy factor. The fact is that we possess the scientific knowledge, the technical expertise, the capital requirements, and all the necessary elements needed to develop energy production for an indefinite future. Moreover, our plenitude of potential power makes the arguments of Meadows irrelevant in the long run, which is just the point where his predictions are supposed to be effective.

The socio-cultural matrix

His predictions are also irrelevant in the short run because he has ignored the fact that our technological age is embedded in a socio-cultural matrix. Although *The Limits to Growth* does take into consideration some nontechnical factors such as the psychological components entering into the birth rate, it ignores the fact that technology functions in a socio-cultural matrix and that we have been developing means for social control and guidance of our technology.

I am not really arguing against *The Limits to Growth* in stressing this point. Professor Meadows and his mentor, the brilliant and respected Jay Forrester, claim that their purpose is to provoke and stimulate society to institute controls over our industrial system. I claim that the social mechanisms are already functioning, some of them in an embryonic stage, and that they neglect these mechanisms in their analysis.

As an historian of technology, I am particularly

offended because they seem to regard technology as an autonomous force, completely separated from man and society. Technology is an integral part of man and society. As a product of human imagination, ingenuity, skill and expertise, it responds to human wants and social needs, and, at the same time, it helps shape our wants and needs. In other words, it is in a very interdependent relationship with society.

Although society has established certain institutions and mechanisms for the guidance and control of its technology, *The Limits to Growth* virtually ignores this fact and simply assumes that technology functions as an independent variable without reference to social norms and institutional control. Indeed, one of the goals of the study is to have us adopt institutional mechanisms to control technology. I say that we already have these, and that we are developing still more. Some of the mechanisms for social control of our industrial base are represented by governmental legislation and administrative agencies. Examples would be the antitrust laws, safety laws, and laws governing the employment of women and minors. Nongovernmental institutions also exercise a certain degree of social control over our industrial system, labor unions being the obvious mechanism.

In the nongovernmental sector we also have the price system. It is a very delicate mechanism, especially when coupled with the profit motive, which is the hallmark of our capitalist society. Indeed, some of the economists who have criticized *The Limits to Growth* place great reliance upon the price mechanism to correct the imbalances which the MIT group envisages. These economists claim that as certain raw materials become scarce, their price will go higher, so that it will no longer be economic to use them—and hence there will be a search for replacement. Thus, they argue, the price system will itself suffice to delay or prevent altogether the exhaustion of natural resources.

While recognizing the value of the price system, I submit that it is not sufficient by itself to avert the dangerous future predicted by *The Limits to Growth*. The price system has two major defects in controlling our technology: first, it sacrifices long-range interest to short-range profits; and second, these profits tend to benefit a few and need not necessarily redound to the benefit of the community as a whole. We have long ago learned that what is good for General Motors might not be good for the rest of the country.

Other social controls are developing, however, and these do not inhibit the good features of the price mechanism. We are now in the process of developing social and institutional mechanisms which will provide effective control and guidance of our technology so that it will be used for the benefit of a wider group in society, preserve our natural environment, and develop the treasure which we leave to posterity. These new socio-political mechanisms go under the general heading of "technology assessment," which attempts to evaluate the social and human consequences of the application of science and technology—before these are applied.

Technology assessment

Man has always assessed the effectiveness of his technology, but his past assessments were confined to seeing if it would murder his enemies more effectively or bring him greater profits. Now we are trying to extend this assessment to second-order and third-order social and human consequences.

We are already familiar with some of the manifestations of this technology-assessment movement. They go under the headings of environmentalism, consumerism, and accountability. For example, the public is beginning to demand that scientists, engineers, business corporations, and government officials be held accountable for the environmental, human, and social consequences of their actions. The passage of the Environmental Quality Control Act and the establishment of the Environmental Protection Agency are demonstrations of the public's concern, as is the stiffening of the Food and Drug Administration, and the recent discussion of a bill for a Consumer Protection Board. The simple fact is that the public is increasingly aroused by the specter of damage to the ecology and environment and is furious about the shoddiness and inadequacy of the consumer products offered by American industry. The legislative and executive arms at all levels of government have been increasingly responsive to this public and consumer sentiment; they are competing with one another to introduce stronger legislation for environmental and consumer protection.

Although technology assessment is still in its infancy, and the presidential election has stalled the passage of a bill establishing an Office of Technology Assessment, it is evident that some kind of governmental mechanism for evaluating the social and human consequences of technical applications will soon be established. Scientists, engineers, and social scientists are beginning to work on the problems of methodology of technology assessment. We can anticipate that such assessments will eventually be applied to scientific discoveries and technical inventions before they are introduced and receive widespread use.

Technology assessment should reaffirm our faith in man and strengthen our faith in democracy. At a time when the Club of Rome implies that we have allowed technology to run amok and ruin our future, technology assessment insists that man is still in control of his destiny. Technology assessment says that man can control the use of his own technology; that human skill, imagination, and creativity can help bring man a better life; and that we are not the playthings of a mindless technology which crushes us underfoot. It means that man is master of his own machine, not its slave.

Technology assessment is also democratic. It does *not* mean that a group of technocrats or meritocrats, or a scientific and technological elite, or the Club of Rome, will make decisions for us. These will be made by the political process, and that, in a democratic system, is where such decisions belong. Democracy allows us the privilege of making mistakes. Technology assessment, however, tells us the options open to us and their possible and probable consequences.

Technology assessment is already being done on a fragmented and piecemeal basis in relation to environmental quality and drug safety. It will soon become a widespread and pervasive activity in American society. As an historian, I view this as part of a great historical current which goes under the heading of "participatory democracy." Much as we might disapprove of some of the manifestations of this trend, the fact is that democracy is extending itself to meet the ideals set forth in our great American Revolution. People are demanding a greater voice in their destinies, and since technology represents an important element in our human experience, they will inevitably demand—and, in a truly democratic society, they will obtain—greater control of their technology. Technology assessment provides a rational means for democratic control and guidance.

I place great faith in technology assessment. If we can utilize it properly, I think that we can avoid the evil consequences which Meadows and his colleagues foresee for our industrial system. This does not mean that the path of the future will be smooth and easy. We will have to cope with environmental blight and ecological difficulties and social maladjustments and resource and energy problems as inevitable and continuing consequences of industrial advance. But it is better to cope with the problems than run away from them, to deal with them rather than ignore them. Above all, we must realize that these problems cannot be resolved by stopping all sources of change, by a moratorium on technological innovation and the cessation of economic growth. Problems caused by our past use, abuse, and misuse of technology cannot be resolved by rolling backward the technological clock.

Ours is a society of so-called "high" technology. We may be no more happy or no more secure than our ancestors, but this is an exciting age in which to live. *The Limits to Growth* has pointed out some of the dangers which might confront us. But I recall the dictum of Alfred North Whitehead: "It is the business of the future to be dangerous." We can accept the risks with composure and confidence if we do not let ourselves be frightened by false alarms which turn us away from growth, if we strengthen our science and technology to meet the challenges of the future, and if we carry on with the task of developing mechanisms and institutions for the control of our technology along socially beneficial lines.

4 | Energy supply as a factor in economic growth

ABRAHAM GERBER

GROWTH IN ENERGY consumption is an essential concomitant of economic growth. The growth in energy consumption broadly reflects the rate of capital accumulation since capital accumulation in large measure consists of equipment designed to harness inanimate energy resources. Significant curtailment of the rate of growth of energy consumption cannot be accomplished, therefore, without curtailment of the rate of capital accumulation and of economic growth. This is not to say that improvements in the efficiency of energy use cannot or should not be sought to the fullest extent possible as a means of moderating the growth in energy consumption. However, these are likely to have only marginal effects on total energy requirements. One may debate whether economic growth itself is desirable, but such growth, to the extent it occurs, will require commensurate growth in energy consumption.

While energy consumption in the United States has risen as the economy has grown, the ratio of energy use per dollar of real GNP has declined. Following a downward trend that began in the 1920s, consumption per dollar of real GNP continued to decline from the end of World War II until 1966. Between 1947 and 1966, GNP (1958 dollars) rose 112.4 percent, energy consumption (trillion Btu) rose 73.3 percent, and energy consumption per dollar of GNP declined at an annual rate of 0.7 percent. This decline in large measure reflected the continuing improvement in the physical efficiency of energy use. Two of the principal sources of efficiency improvement in this period were the railroads and the electric utilities. The conversion from the coal-fired steam engine to the oil-fired diesel represented a major advance in the efficiency of energy use which was completed by the mid-1950s. The efficiency of thermal generation of electricity improved throughout the period as the average heat input per kilowatt-hour generated fell by about one-third, from 15,600 Btu per kilowatt-hour to a low of 10,399 Btu per kilowatt-hour. At the same time, the share of total energy converted to electricity increased from 13.4 percent to 21.3 percent.

Since 1966 a change in these trends appears to have taken place, and a fairly sharp increase in the energy/GNP ratio has occurred. From 1966 to 1970 the energy/GNP ratio rose from 86.5 thousand Btu per dollar (1958 dollars) to 95.6 thousand Btu per dollar, an increase of over 10 percent, which raised the ratio back to the level of the early 1950s. Whether the trend reversal in the energy/GNP ratio will persist or the ratio will resume its long-term decline remains uncertain at present. However, resumption of a significant decline in the energy/GNP ratio in the near future appears doubtful for several reasons.

The trend of improved thermal efficiency of electric generation appears to have reached a plateau where it is likely to remain at least for the next several years. In the period 1947-1959, thermal efficiency improved at an average annual rate of 3.26 percent. Between 1959 and 1966 the average annual rate of improvement was only 0.73 percent. Between 1966 and 1970 thermal efficiency deteriorated and the heat rate rose from 10,399 Btu per kilowatt-hour generated to 10,508 Btu. This deterioration in the efficiency of electric generation occurred for several reasons. With present technology the maximum feasible level of efficiency is in the neighborhood of 8,500 Btu per kilowatt-hour. As this level is approached, the difference between the average efficiency of existing generating plants and new plants decreases and the effect of new plants, on the average, diminishes. At the same time, delays in new generating capacity in the past several years have made necessary the more intensive operation of older, less efficient plants, which has adversely affected average efficiency. In addition, it has also been necessary to install, and use more intensively than would be preferred, gas-turbine peaking capacity with thermal efficiencies comparable to the lower average efficiency that prevailed at the end of World War II. This, too, has adversely affected thermal efficiency in the last four years. Environmental constraints, which have necessitated the installation of more effluent control equipment such as cooling towers and stack-gas treatment devices, have also reduced thermal efficiency. These constraints have also led to greater use of oil, with its inherently lower thermal efficiency, in place of coal. Finally, as the nuclear share of new capacity increases, the favorable effect of new thermal capacity on average efficiency is reduced. These factors are likely to continue to affect changes in thermal efficiency. In addition, further adverse effects on thermal efficiency can be expected as additional environmental protection technologies, such as stack-gas desulfurization, are superimposed on existing technology.

Another possible deterrent to resumption of the decline in the energy/GNP ratio is the growth in energy use for purposes which are not directly reflected in GNP. In the period 1947-1970, household and commercial energy consumption (the data do not permit a ready breakdown between household and commercial) rose by

170 percent from 8,731 trillion Btu to 23,579 trillion Btu, and consumption per capita rose 91 percent from 60.6 million Btu to 115.8 million Btu. The share of total energy consumption in the United States accounted for by the household and commercial sectors rose over this period from a little under 27 percent to over 34 percent.

Although a breakdown between the household and commercial sectors is not readily available for total energy, separate data are available for electricity. Residential consumption of electricity rose 864.2 percent between 1947 and 1970 compared with a total increase in electricity consumption of 539.5 percent. Residential consumption increased from 21.3 percent to 32.2 percent of total electricity consumption. Problems of inconsistencies over time in the classification between commercial and industrial customers make the data for commercial use less than precise for purposes of trend comparisons. Nevertheless, they provide an appropriate indication of the shifts which have occurred. In the 1947-1970 period, commercial use of electricity rose 694.5 percent, and its share of total electricity consumption rose from 18 percent to 23 percent. Residential and commercial use of electricity increased from 39 percent to 55 percent of total electricity consumption.

This increase in electricity use by the household and commercial sectors to improve the amenities of the home and working environments has led to a substantial increase in energy use without accompanying GNP growth. For example, the rapid growth of electricity consumption for air conditioning, while it may over time lead to higher productivity and GNP, is not directly and concurrently reflected in the GNP data. Similarly, the use of energy for the operation of television sets, home laundry equipment, or computers may enhance the quality of life or increase productivity, but also is not reflected directly and immediately in the GNP measure.

Indeed, in the case of the home laundry equipment, the transfer of laundry service from the commercial laundry to the home results in an actual subtraction from GNP without a corresponding reduction in energy use.

Such energy uses can be expected to continue rising as per capita income continues to rise, and particularly as those presently at the lower income levels improve their relative income position. Some indication of the potential for such growth in energy consumption is indicated by the results of surveys conducted by the Department of Commerce in January 1967 and July 1970. The 1967 survey revealed that only 4.3 percent of the households with annual income under $3,000 owned an air conditioner while 28.5 percent of those with annual income between $7,500 and $9,999 owned one. Of those households with annual income of $15,000 and over, 44.9 percent owned an air conditioner. Although the survey does not indicate the number of air conditioners owned per household or the number of central whole-house air conditioners, it is a reasonable expectation that not only does the percent of households owning air conditioners increase as household income increases, but that the number of air conditioners per household and the number of central air conditioners also increase. The 1970 survey indicated that only 3 percent of households with annual income under $3,000 owned dishwashers while 15 percent of those with annual income of $7,500-$9,999 and 71 percent of those with incomes of $25,000 and over owned dishwashers. For clothes driers the percentages were 11.8 percent, 49.7 percent and 81.9 percent, respectively. In the case of color TV sets, the percentages were 13.1 percent, 45.5 percent, and 73.4 percent. These percentages represent wide disparities in the availability of the appliances to consumers at various income levels and provide a rough indication of the potential for growth in energy consumption for presently known applications which can be expected to result from raising the incomes of those now at the lower income levels. In the period 1961-1970, for example, we estimate that color TV, electric clothes driers (which account for about 70 percent of all clothes driers in homes), and air conditioning combined accounted for over one-fourth of the total growth of residential consumption of electricity, which, in the aggregate, increased 75.8 percent in this period.

Further evidence regarding the important effects of rising income levels on growth in energy use, especially for those presently at the lower income levels, is provided by data on electricity consumption and per capita income in Philadelphia and surrounding suburbs. Average annual electricity consumption of suburban residential customers of Philadelphia Electric Company in 1970 was 7,479 kilowatt-hours compared with only 4,600 kilowatt-hours by customers within the city. This conforms with the results of an earlier study carried out at NERA on the basis of 1967 data. In this study we found that for the twenty cities in the United States with the largest core populations served by investor-owned electric utilities, the average annual consumption of electricity by residential customers within each city was significantly below that of the same utility's customers outside each city. Since for each utility the residential rates were the same for customers both inside and outside the city, price could not have been a determinant of the difference. In New York City, for example, average consumption in Manhattan was less than half the average in Westchester County. Furthermore, despite higher rates, average consumption in Westchester County was one-third above the average for the city of Chicago. Analyses of these and other data suggest that differences in income levels and in housing characteristics (in part related to income levels) are the principal factors accounting for the differences between urban and suburban electricity use. The differences appeared to be influenced especially by the proportion of single-family, owner-occupied homes, and even comparisons among central cities indicated a close relationship between this factor and average annual use of electricity. Some evidence of the relationship between energy consumption and price was obtained during this study by a survey of apartment dwellers in New York City. The survey revealed that the percent of apartment dwellers having various consuming appliances was the same for the group who paid their own utility bills and for those whose utility bills were included in the rent.

The data for Philadelphia provide further indication of the effect of rising income on energy use. For the city of Philadelphia, average annual electricity use per residential customer increased 88 percent in the 1960-1970 decade compared with growth of 63 percent in the suburban area served by Philadelphia Electric Company. Rough estimates were made of 1960 per capita income (based on the *1960 Census of Population*) to determine per capita income for each district and division of Philadelphia Electric Company. Per capita income in Philadelphia in 1960 was $1,580 compared with $2,221 in the suburban divisions. Within the city those areas with per capita income below the city average also had electricity consumption per residential customer below the city average and a more rapid rate of growth in electricity consumption per customer in the 1960-1970 decade. The same relationships were found in the suburban areas, although at higher absolute levels. Furthermore, the average annual consumption in the suburban division with the lowest average use was above the average for the district within the city with the highest average use. However, the district within the city with the lowest growth rate for the decade had a faster growth rate in average annual residential consumption than the fastest growing suburban division. Over the decade the relative gap in average annual consumption between residential customers within the city and in the suburbs narrowed. In 1960, average use in the suburbs exceeded the city average by 38.1 percent, but by 1970 it was 28.6 percent. However, in absolute quantities the gap widened from 870 kilowatt-hours to 1,317 kilowatt-hours, although by 1970 average use in the city had risen 88 percent and exceeded the 1960 suburban average by almost 40 percent. The slowest growth over the decade, 60 percent, occurred in the three suburban divisions which in 1960 already had the highest average use. These data indicate that in the Philadelphia area, at least, the more rapid rates of increase in electric energy use are occurring among those at the lower income and energy-use levels.

Despite the contention by some that the rapid growth in energy use by industry, and especially energy-intensive industry, has been a major factor in causing the rapid growth in total energy use, the industrial sector has shown the least rapid growth. In the 1947-1970 period, total energy consumption by industry increased by about 90 percent, from 15,090 trillion Btu to 28,556 trillion Btu, and the share of total energy declined from about 46 percent in 1947 to a little over 41 percent. At the same time, the index of private nonfarm output (1957-1959=100) rose 142.5 percent from 67.6 to 163.9, and output per man-hour almost doubled from 74.1 to 134.6. Energy consumption as a ratio of the FRB Index of Manufacturing and Mining Production declined from 223.2 trillion Btu in 1947 to 174.2 trillion Btu in 1970. It would appear, therefore, that energy is being used more efficiently in industry. At least there does not appear to be any sign of significant deterioration in the efficiency of energy use by industry.

The *1967 Census of Manufactures* provides the latest comprehensive data on energy use in manufacturing. A comparison of these data with the *1958 Census of Manufactures* shows that for the 29 four-digit industry classifications which are energy-intensive (i.e., those with cost of purchased fuel and electricity equal to 4 percent or more of the value of shipments in 1967), value added increased only 36.6 percent between the two census years compared with 85.1 percent growth for all manufacturing. There is also some evidence in the data that the rate of growth in output may be inversely correlated with the rate of growth in energy consumption per unit of output. Data limitations in the Census did not permit this analysis of the relationship between the rate of growth in output and energy consumption on a four-digit industry basis. The two-digit industry classifications could obscure significant shifts within each of the two-digit classifications. Nevertheless, it is of some interest that from 1958 to 1967 manufacturing output increased 75.7 percent while energy consumption per unit of output (as measured by the FRB index) declined 20 percent. In part this may reflect the slower-than-average growth rate for the four-digit energy-intensive industry components of the two-digit industry groups. The regression equation between the percentage increase in production and energy use per unit of output based on two-digit industry classifications yields a correlation coefficient of -0.72.

With regard to electricity consumption by industry, the data indicate similar trends. Industrial use of electricity rose 394.6 percent in the 1947-1970 period and the share of total electricity consumption declined from 53.2 percent to 41.1 percent.

Although the long-term downward trend in energy consumption per dollar of real GNP appears to have come to a halt, it is not yet clear whether a long-term reversal of the trend is beginning. The household and commercial sectors have been increasing their share of total energy use, and this is likely to continue. This will result in growth in energy consumption without concomitant growth in GNP. However, this is in part a result of the inadequacies in our measurement of GNP. Industrial consumption of energy per unit of output has been declining, but this decline is likely to slow as more energy is consumed for environmental protection without being reflected in the output measure. The upward trend in the electric share of total energy consumption can be expected to continue at the same time that the improvements in thermal efficiency appear to have reached a plateau or even reversed. In part this is also the expected result of increased energy use for environmental protection. Thus, for both manufacturing and electric generation some deterioration in the efficiency of energy use may appear because the statistics do not incorporate the value of environmental protection in the product. In any case, the indications are that the energy requirements per dollar of GNP are unlikely to decline and will at best remain stable. Thus, while energy consumption has increased in the past at a slower rate than GNP, the present outlook is for increases in energy requirements at a rate at least equal to the growth of GNP. At the same time, there is growing concern that the supply of energy in the United States is inadequate and that the country faces an "energy crisis."

Such fears regarding the exhaustion of energy resources have been expressed previously. As long ago as 1865 the distinguished English economist Stanley Jevons, in his book *The Coal Question*, projected the decline of the English economy as a result of the imminent exhaustion of its coal resources. Indeed, following World War II there was serious discussion of "carrying coals to Newcastle." Within a few years, however, the English faced the problem of a coal surplus. Similarly, the nations of Western Europe were deeply distressed following World War II by the prospect that fuel shortages, especially of coal, would limit their economic growth. As in England, within a relatively brief period the problems of a coal surplus emerged.

The so-called "energy crisis" in the United States differs from these other circumstances in several important respects. First, it is not the result of any imminent exhaustion of energy resources. The present concern over supply stringency and the rising price of energy has been the result of self-imposed limitations on the types of fuel to be used in order to achieve environmental objectives. Because of the relatively brief time period within which the air- and water-quality standards and pollution-abatement regulations have emerged, there has been insufficient time to make the technological adjustments necessary to overcome the fuel limitations they have imposed. Second, unlike previous experiences with impending energy shortages, the opportunities for restoring energy abundance are numerous. For example, successful development of coal and/or stack-gas desulfurization technology would expand the usable coal resources manyfold. The development of coal-gasification technology would make possible assurance of adequate long-term gas supplies. The use of dry cooling towers, now under development, would free electric-power generation from dependence on large quantities of cooling water. For the longer term, breeder reactors, nuclear fusion, and hydrogen fuel cells offer the prospect of almost limitless energy supplies. These latter technologies, however, require conversion to electricity.

It is by no means clear that the present "energy crisis" confronts the nation with a long-term problem. To the contrary, the indications are that it is a relatively short-term problem which, in large measure, has been self-imposed and for which solutions are visible. Nevertheless, as is sometimes the case, there appears to be a tendency in the present energy circumstances to adopt immediate crisis measures as though the short-term problem were in actuality a long-term condition. In response to the current stringency in energy supply and the concern for environmental quality, it is being widely suggested that growth in energy use be curtailed. This is sometimes coupled with the suggestion that economic growth be curtailed. However, the interrelationship between energy growth and economic growth and the fact that curtailment in one implies curtailment in the other are often not recognized or, at least, are not acknowledged.

While it may be interesting to speculate on the implications of a static economy, it is highly unlikely that a significant slowing of the rate of economic expansion will be acceptable, at least for the balance of this century. Despite encouraging signs of a slowing of the birth rate toward the point of zero population growth, population will continue to grow for the next several decades even if this rate is maintained. In addition to providing for this growth, the economy will also have to provide rising per capita income especially for those segments of the population now at income levels far below the current average. It has been suggested that this objective could be achieved by income redistribution. However, without revolutionary change in social and economic institutions this appears to be a remote possibility. Redistribution of the growth in the nation's product may offer a feasible means of improving the relative positions of those at the lower income levels, but peaceful economic and social restructuring to achieve voluntary redistribution of a static GNP is unlikely to be attainable. To raise the incomes of all to acceptable levels in the absence of economic growth would require reaching too deeply into the middle income levels and redistributing income away from too large a segment of the population. Therefore, growth in per capita income will be necessary. This will affect the growth in energy consumption in two ways: first, growth in energy consumption will be required to achieve the increase in productivity required to increase per capita income; second, as per capita income rises, consumers will increase their energy consumption. Improved housing, for example, is likely to be accompanied by increased energy consumption, and even such aesthetic enjoyments as camping in the woods are likely to require energy for transportation.

Proposals to curtail energy use as a means of resolving both the energy-resource and environmental problems have tended to focus on electric energy, perhaps because it is the most rapidly growing form of energy consumption. Here again, analysis appears to indicate a contrary response. From the point of view of environmental impact, electric-energy use permits the transfer of fuel combustion with its accompanying effluent from the point of ultimate energy use, usually in densely populated areas, to more remote, sparsely populated areas. The concentration of fuel use in large central stations also affords greater administrative as well as technological opportunities for controlling effluents than would be the case when fuel use is widely dispersed among large numbers of small users. Finally, the development of nuclear generation eliminates the problems of gaseous and particulate emissions. Although the problem of thermal emissions is more severe with a nuclear plant than with a fossil-fuel plant, the technology for its solution is available.

Nuclear generation also offers the means for circumventing the problem of energy-resource depletion. Conversion of energy use from direct fuel use to electric energy provides the most effective means for circumventing the threat of energy shortage. Electricity can be produced by any of the fossil fuels, uranium, fusion and geothermal steam, and even the very long-run prospect of solar energy (if, indeed, it is a prospect) is likely to be useful principally through conversion to electricity. Furthermore, our most abundant fossil fuel, coal, is unlikely to be an important source of energy unless it is either gasified, liquefied or converted to electricity. Nuclear fuel is also of little value as a source of energy unless it is converted to electricity. The longer-term technological prospects for avoiding energy-resource limitations on economic growth, breeder reactors and nuclear fusion, suggest accelerated electrification of energy consumption, i.e., the substitution of electricity for direct fuel use, as the desirable course for avoiding energy-resource depletion.

Because electricity and the fuels are substitutable in a wide range of energy uses, arbitrary curtailment of growth in electricity consumption would be likely to induce a shift toward the direct use of fuel, principally oil and gas. This would, therefore, tend to exacerbate the "energy crisis" and could even worsen the environmental impact of energy use.

Although electrification clearly could provide the means for broadening fuel-resource alternatives and thereby relieve the pressure of fuel-resource stringency, the contrary argument is now being advanced that electric-energy consumption should be curtailed because it is less efficient in its use of fuel than direct fuel use. Controversies are now developing over measurements of the relative physical efficiencies (i.e., Btu of fuel per unit of output) of electricity and direct fuel use in various applications. These controversies are irrelevant because they are confined to physical efficiency and ignore criteria of economic efficiency. One may question whether existing prices properly reflect the costs, including scarcity, of electricity and the fuels. However, to the extent that they do, the appropriate measure of efficiency is cost. To compel the use of the physically more efficient energy source, if relative prices indicate that this source is more scarce and costly, represents a misallocation of resources. Furthermore, in choosing among energy sources, the costs of all complementary inputs, including labor, associated with the use of each fuel must be included, since the objective should be the economically efficient use of all resources. This principle extends beyond the direct comparison among energy sources to comparison among energy-intensive and non-energy-intensive processes and products. Arbitrary curtailment of energy-intensive products such as aluminum, for example, may lead to shifts toward the use of more costly and scarcer lumber resources. To the extent that prices reflect these relationships they signal the choices. The consequences of arbitrarily circumventing these signals to achieve physical conservation of a single resource which may be the immediate focus of attention are insufficiently understood, and their ramifications could have serious adverse long-term effects. They may even result in greater use of the resource whose conservation was intended when the entire matrix of interindustry relationships works its way through. This is not to say that improvement in the efficiency of energy use is not desirable. But it must be based on the balance among economic alternatives. Improvements in physical efficiency which result in higher costs suggest that the single resource is being conserved at the expense of other, more valuable (or scarcer) resources (assuming that prices in the marketplace properly reflect costs and resource scarcity). From the point of view of economic welfare the result is likely to be deterioration, both short term and long term, rather than enhancement.

It appears that, barring a decision to curtail economic growth, efforts to significantly curtail growth in energy consumption are likely to be unrealistic exercises in futility. Rather than focusing attention on the means to curtail energy consumption or on irrelevant arguments over the relative physical efficiencies of the several energy sources, efforts need to be made to find ways in which to accommodate energy requirements to the available energy resources and to the other social and economic objectives we seek to achieve. This will involve the determination of appropriate technological and economic research directions and policies which avoid distortions in the relative prices and supply and demand for the several energy sources.

In shaping energy-resource policies we should keep in mind that we cannot expect to resolve all problems for all time. Indeed, it would be arrogant on our part to believe we could do so. We have the obligation, and hopefully the capability, to resolve the problems of today and perhaps of tomorrow; but for the day after tomorrow conditions will differ, new technologies and new solutions not yet visualized will become feasible, and, based on our achievements, new generations with capabilities at least equal to ours will be able to build beyond anything we may now visualize. Our responsibility is to find a way to pass through the next two or three decades without foreclosing the options available to the next generation and to convey to that generation a viable economy. We probably cannot expect to do more, but we must not do less.

5 | Growth and environmental problems of noncapitalist nations

MARSHALL I. GOLDMAN

NOW THAT IT IS intellectually acceptable to devote a conference to what was until recently the indiscreet subject of zero economic growth (ZEG), a major question remains: If we decide we want it, how do we get it? For many the answer is clear—abolish capitalism.

For those who advocate such action, the reasoning is not hard to follow. ZEG seems to be the only way we can control pollution and preserve our environment. But ZEG is impossible in a capitalist society. In the view of such critics, the lust for profit fostered under the capitalist system necessitates ever-expanding growth in markets and production, and this in turn inevitably brings pollution. Thus, in the words of Douglas Dowd at San Jose State College, "You can't undo this mess [pollution] under the capitalist system. The scope of the environmental problems is now enormous—they can only be taken care of in a planned economy."[1] Barry Commoner has a somewhat similar reaction. He too feels that the private enterprise system depends on continued growth to perpetuate itself, whereas this is not necessarily the case in "socialist economies [where] there is no theoretical demand for continuous growth."[2]

Whatever the theory, the reality is something else. A study of pollution and economic growth in countries with communist regimes as well as in state-run economies of the developing world reveals little evidence, and even less theory, to indicate that ZEG and environmental control are any easier for communist or socialist factory managers than for their American counterparts. The fact that the state owns all the means of production and issues annual and five-year plans guarantees nothing. The fact that the private enterprise system is ill suited for ZEG and that it has not proven to be particularly well equipped to cope with pollution does not automatically mean that a state-owned economy will do better. It generally turns out that the leaders and managers in Soviet-type systems as well as those in the developing countries must contend not only with all the forces that exist in the United States but with a few more as well.[3] Compared to the United States, there is depressingly little enthusiasm in such countries for ZEG or even for environmental control.

Reality and the pressures for growth in the noncapitalist world

In our yearning for improvement over what we know, we frequently turn to what we do not know on the assumption that, since conditions can hardly be worse than they are here, they might be better elsewhere. It is true, of course, that individuals and firms in capitalist countries such as the United States have always been concerned about increasing profits and incomes, but until recently this has generally been on a micro or individual basis. Before World War II there was very little emphasis in the United States or the capitalist world on national economic growth. It was not until the mid-twentieth century that Simon Kuznets managed to turn the concept of GNP into something that

decent people would talk about around the dinner table
or in presidential campaigns. Prior to that, it was a
historical curiosity, and naturally there was no such
thing as ongoing quarterly and yearly statements of
GNP. Thus, until relatively recently, only a very few
in the United States knew or cared what GNP was. Of
course, there has always been a desire for national
power, but that was a military, not an economic, concept. In fact, there are many instances, such as early
nineteenth-century Russia, in which a country was an
impressive military power but had little or no economic
power. Given our current neuroses about growth, it
seems difficult to believe, but our national worship of
economic growth above all else is relatively new.

The Soviet quest for growth

What we forget is that it is the Soviets as much
as anyone who are responsible for the world's emphasis
on macroeconomic growth. Contrary to the teachings of
Karl Marx, the revolution took place in an underdeveloped country. Upon assuming power, the Soviets sought
to build up their economic strength and industrialize as
rapidly as possible. To do this, they looked about for
work stimuli. They sought some way to translate their
ambitions into concrete goals toward which they could
strive. If it had been a meaningful or useful concept at
the time, they doubtless would have set their sights in
terms of specified increases in GNP. But since they began their search in the late 1920s, the most suitable
device they could think of was to establish targets in
physical output for specific commodities. It was upon
this foundation, therefore, that the system of annual
and five-year plans was built.

Since 1928 it has been the dream of every Soviet

manager and government official to increase his output by more than the specified target. The stress on increased output and growth has permeated the society from the factory floor to the Politburo ceiling. With all the boasting about economic growth in the USSR, it was only natural that concern about economic growth should be heightened in the noncommunist world. It is entirely possible, of course, that after the trauma of the Great Depression and the chaos of World War II, the noncommunist world would have set off in pursuit of high growth rates even without the goading of the Soviet Union. Nonetheless, if the Soviets did not create the international mania for growth, certainly they did more to nourish and emphasize it than anyone else.

Not only was growth made the keystone of Soviet policy, but because of peculiarities in the nature of Soviet ideology and institutions, the growth that did take place was usually hard on the environment. This is an almost inevitable by-product as long as Marxian ideology holds that labor is the source of all value. To the extent that the Russians have adhered to this doctrine, they have tended to treat natural resources as free goods. This makes it difficult for Soviet leaders to protect the environment, even when they have the best of intentions. Economists have been concerned for some time about the tendency in noncommunist economies to treat water and air as semi-free or free goods. The consequences are bound to be more severe when all raw materials are treated the same way, as they have been for many years in the USSR. When anything is free, there is a tendency to consume excess quantities of it without regard for future consequences. But as with free love, there is a limit to how much of a country's air and water can be consumed. After a time there is the risk of exhaustion. In the USSR, natural resources, as well as air and water, are misallocated in this way.

Any pricing policy which values ideology more highly than the environment leads to an economy with a production function that is material-intensive. This is reflected in the Soviet Union by the very low recovery rates of most mining and drilling operations. Many mines and oil wells in the USSR have only a 50 percent recovery rate.[4] The rest of the oil or ore is left in the ground or discarded as spoils. This not only results in faster than normal exhaustion of resources, but it also increases the pollution problem, since many of the spoils end up in bodies of water as silt, acid, oil, or salt brine.

Although they may be aware of what is happening, Soviet mine and well operators are virtually helpless to do anything to prevent such wastes. Their actions are dictated by the system. The mine or well manager seeks to hold down his labor and machinery costs. He is not concerned about real land or mineral costs, which from his perspective are nonexistent. Therefore, whenever the ore content of a deposit begins to fall, the manager will move on to an adjacent site where a ruble expenditure on labor and machinery will yield a higher return. Incidentally, this raw-material-intensive attitude is also reflected in Soviet willingness to export vast quantities of raw materials. The Soviets are major exporters of ores and petroleum products and they are continually seeking markets, with little regard to the fact that such materials will be even more valuable in the future.[5]

Soviet factory managers tend to operate in the same way as mine and well operators. Even when funds are set aside for pollution control, factory managers are tempted not to use them for the intended purpose. Faced with the constant exhortation to increase their production, Soviet factory managers (just like their noncommunist counterparts) are unenthusiastic about spending money on anything that does not contribute toward an increase in output. If pollution control causes a reduction in output, a manager's attitude will be even more negative. In fact, in the Soviet Union it has been discovered that, as often as not, funds allocated for pollution control either are not spent or are diverted so that increased production rather than decreased pollution is the result.[6] There might be less temptation for such misappropriation if a higher value were assigned to virgin raw materials or if prices were attached to clear water and air and charges were assessed for polluting them. Then the factory manager might find that by installing pollution-control equipment and by the careful processing of raw materials, he could actually make money by recycling and husbanding expensive resources. In other words, conceivably he could make enough money by recycling and conserving to offset the penalties that accompany a failure to increase production as planned. As imperfect as the pricing mechanism in capitalist countries may be from an environmental point of view, the idea of free natural resources is at least one shortcoming that we are spared. The value of raw materials may well be understated in the capitalist countries, but except for water and air, such resources are usually not treated as free goods.

Ideology is not the only thing that affects the operation of the pricing process in communist societies. In addition to questions of doctrine, there are also simple operational problems. While no price system perfectly reflects economic costs and demand and supply pressures, the Soviet pricing system has so far proven to be particularly cumbersome and unresponsive. Complaints about the operation of the Soviet system are endemic. For example, prices are rarely changed. It is not unusual for price lists in the country to be ten or fifteen years old. Among other reasons for such inflexibility is the fact that more frequent changes are bureaucratically very complex and difficult to implement and administer. With changes so infrequent, it is only to be expected that price relationships between products and components will become artificial and unresponsive. Thus even agreed-upon costs are frequently not reflected in prices. A good example of this occurred in 1967 when a major revision of wholesale prices was made while retail prices were held fixed so as not to upset the Soviet consumer.

Recently some Soviet economists have come to recognize the wastefulness of such a system. As a result, some support has developed for changes in the pricing mechanism. Since the Soviet price system is only partially dependent on market forces, it is conceivable that the Russians could go all the way and decree that raw materials should reflect not only the rental and depletion costs we are accustomed to in the West, but social costs as well. Stranger things have happened in the USSR. As one hopeful sign, there is a report that the costs of restoring the soil were included in the price of ore from a manganese strip mine in the Ukraine. So far, however, this is the only instance I can find of such a practice, and the manner in which the operation was described seems to indicate its uniqueness.[7]

Certainly there will have to be a fundamental repudiation of basic doctrine before the Russians come to value their natural resources even as highly as do noncommunist countries. There is no evidence that the Russians are anywhere near such a decision. In fact, even after that mythical day when the Soviet Union manages to overtake and surpass the United States (shortly it may be surprised to learn that it is not just the USA, but also Japan that must be overtaken), there is no reason to believe that the Russians will lose their passion for growth. The Russian people have become increasingly bourgeois in their tastes, and they show no sign of giving up their quest for a better material life.

Thus, theoretically, mechanically, ideologically, and individually, the notion of ZEG seems to be ill suited for a communist country such as the USSR. And without ZEG, the chances for environmental control in the Soviet Union are no better than they are in the noncommunist countries. For that matter, given the operation of the Soviet price and incentive systems, there is considerable reason to doubt the effectiveness of a pollution control program in the Soviet Union even with ZEG.

The developing countries

The emphasis on growth in the less developed countries is just as intense. This is true irrespective of whether the leader calls his country capitalist, socialist, feudal, monarchist, or anarchist. In almost every instance the prime objective of countries in the Afro-Asian bloc is to increase their GNP and to do it rapidly. Pious warnings about what lies ahead if every country on the planet continues to grow at annual rates of 5 percent per capita are cast aside as deceitful. If anything, the less developed countries see their GNPs slipping farther behind those of the developed countries.[8] This increases their frustration and their feeling that the richer countries are, in fact, trying to prevent their industrialization and deny them the benefits the rich have enjoyed. Arguments for ZEG, no matter how they are presented, are viewed in this same context.

The hostility toward environmental control is almost as intense. In fact, some regard environmental controls as synonymous with ZEG. As they see it, requiring pollution control will increase their costs of production, which will make it all but impossible to break into established markets. At the extreme, the argument for banning the production and sale of DDT is viewed as an effort at genocide. It may be that the peregrine falcons and bald eagles are threatened, but to those who suffered the massive ravages of malaria before the use of DDT, such considerations are unimportant. Moreover, if an Indian is asked to choose between a life expectancy of 21 with malaria and no DDT or a life expectancy of 60 without malaria but with DDT in his fatty tissue and dead falcons and eagles, there is little doubt as to what his choice will be.

For planners in the less developed countries, the challenge is to grow. With growth, they argue, will come an increase in capabilities that, in turn, will make it possible to set aside some resources for environmental control. Unfortunately, there is considerable truth in the comment that only the affluent can afford to control their effluent. For most of the less developed countries, affluence can be most easily attained by selling off whatever natural resources are available. First of all, many of the more wealthy nations have already exhausted the richest deposits in their own countries and must now look abroad. Second, raw materials are the most salable and competitive commodities at the disposal of the less developed countries. In a sense, raw materials are their ticket to industrialization. To those for whom there is but a brief tomorrow or none at all, the challenge is to see how much they can realize today. They have no patience with those who warn of the danger of selling their grandchildren's inheritance and the need to preserve existing natural resources. In the minds of the leaders of the less developed countries, the industrialization to be financed through the sale of raw materials will be an even better inheritance.

The argument of the more developed nations that the ecological systems in the less developed ones can withstand even less wear and tear than the systems in the temperate and more stable climates is not very compelling to those who seek higher income levels. Nor are the planners intimidated by fears of a serious ecological blunder as our Pandora's box of technology is opened wider and wider. If anything, all these pressures merely make them highly suspicious of rich environmentalists who continually urge them to ban or restrict enterprises (both private and public) which seek to develop the raw materials, labor, and industry of their countries. Why, they ask, should they be prevented from doing what their counterparts in the north did only a few decades ago? In fact, many planners in the less developed countries view the increasing insistence on pollution control in the north as an unmixed blessing. It has become easier and cheaper for many northern industries to relocate in the less developed countries rather than build the expensive pollution-control equipment that would otherwise be necessary if they were to stay in the north. To the less developed countries, the protests from the north are merely a disguised attempt to prevent the migration of jobs and industry. As the planning minister of Brazil put it, "Brazil can become the importer of pollution." "Why not?" he asked. "We have a lot left to pollute." The developed countries of the world, especially Japan, do not. Moreover, if Brazil does not welcome industrial investment from the developed countries, another developing country will.[9]

Rich proponents of no growth stand easily accused of hypocrisy. This kind of dispute is not limited to the international arena. Such differences frequently exist between neighbors within the same country. As an unemployed resident of Maine commented when asked how he felt about opposition to plans for an oil refinery in his neighborhood, "What right do these conservationists from Boston have to oppose the building of this refinery and the jobs it will bring us? They want to preserve us in our natural underdeveloped and impoverished state while they make lots of money in their dirty city. It doesn't seem to bother them that they want one thing for themselves and another thing for us and that we will have to stay poor to make it possible."

Redistribution

Calls from the developed and rich to halt "progress" by the underdeveloped and poor have induced counterproposals by the poor and radical. One that is growing in intensity is for a redistribution of resources and wealth. Thus, if there is to be ZEG, it should be a net result for the world as a whole. In this way the poor would be able to increase their share because resources would be diverted from the rich. While this would produce greater equity, it is not clear how much it would improve the environment.

Let us assume that there is a redistribution of income. Certainly lower income in the United States would cause a sharp fall in the demand for major appliances such as air conditioners and second automobiles. Yet the increasing use of automobiles in Western Europe and Japan and now the USSR suggests that as the poor countries become richer, they will eagerly seek to take up the slack created by the drop in American consumption. In fact, almost all the world's major automobile producers are gearing up for the Asian market, which they feel will be the biggest market yet. We know that the elasticity of income and the marginal propensity to consume are much higher in the less developed countries than in the richer countries. Therefore, it is unlikely that the world demand for consumer goods and appliances will level off or drop much if income should be taken away from Americans and redistributed to the poorer areas of the world. Redistribution may provide some relief, but if the strain on the environment is at all eased, it will probably be due to the fact that in the richer countries of the world the consumption of services is growing faster than the consumption of goods.

It has also been proposed that the nationalization of resources will do much to reduce the thoughtless exploitation and waste of raw materials that presently prevails in so much of the developing world. Those who advocate such a step reason that once the resources are controlled by people who live in the area and the foreigners are dispossessed, the best interests of the area and its resources will become the main determinant of action.[10] Undoubtedly there is room for improvement, and a change in perspective could help. Nonetheless, the evidence so far is not altogether clear. First there is the experience with Soviet nationalization in the USSR. That, as we saw, has not ended thoughtless exploitation. In fact, the Russians themselves are now seeking to exploit raw materials in the developing countries to supplement their own stocks.[11] Most of the instances of nationalization that have occurred outside the USSR are not much more promising. If anything, after nationalization the new native management usually seeks to increase production. They do not always succeed, as, for example, in Chile, but the failure is not due to any lack of spirit or effort. Indeed, often one of the criticisms of the former foreign companies is that they held back on their investment and production. This was the charge against the foreign companies in Libya and Iraq, and the clear implication was that after nationalization the output of the oil fields would be increased.[12] This hardly reflects the spirit of ZEG, not to mention concern for the environment.

Conceivably the day may arrive when the leaders and citizens of a country may decide to forgo growth for theoretical as well as pragmatic reasons.

Thus far, however, the prospects still seem rather dim. For a time it looked as if the Chinese might turn their backs on material growth in exchange for the spiritual growth that seemed to be the goal of the Cultural Revolution. Mao bitterly attacked those who pursued none but the material pleasures. The planners and managers who advocated economic growth and increased production were literally sacked, and some were lucky to escape with their lives. Unfortunately for the environment, the Cultural Revolution was short-lived. Once it was over the Chinese resumed their pursuit of material happiness and economic growth, although they profess that, in their quest, they will not forsake pollution control.

Even during the high point of the Cultural Revolution, however, there was reason to question just how much of Mao's campaign was dictated by concern for the environment and how much by concern for Mao's own personal ideology. Thus, through it all, China continued with her atomic testing in the atmosphere. Of course, until 1963 we did the same thing, and on a larger scale. Our attempt to manipulate the weather and our use of herbicides in Indochina are also a blot on our record. Yet contrary to what some medical idealists would like to believe, the continued Chinese atomic tests and the Egyptian use of poison gas in Yemen suggest that the transfer of power from the rich to the poor does not necessarily guarantee saner societies or more care for the environment.

Overtly, at least, Tanzania continues to reject the worldly ways of industrialization and urbanization. It is still dedicated to seeking a more harmonious union with nature and its agrarian traditions. With the urging of President Julius Nyerere, the government is seeking to encourage the peasants to remain in the countryside and live a self-sufficient agrarian life centered around a type of farming cooperative and self-help village called

UJAMAA. It is too early to tell how successful and how pure its efforts have been.[13] It remains to be seen, however, what will happen if Tanzania's African neighbors manage to industrialize and increase their incomes. Can the Tanzanians hold their appetites in check, or will they, as others before them, seek to keep up with their neighbors?

The planet and the failure of economic systems and theory

The prospects for the planet are not very promising. Hunger for growth is not limited to any one country or system. Of course, inadvertently an enterprise or country may have a no-growth record. In a lighter moment, this may be regarded as a step forward. In an effort to reassure his stockholders, a company president in a recent *New Yorker* cartoon was shown trying to explain his chart of constant sales by saying, "And so we here at Ultronics take great pride in announcing that we are the first American corporation to achieve zero economic growth." For the presidents of most countries and corporations, this would not be an occasion for humor.

Given existing economic institutions and techniques, it is hard to see how any economic system can deal adequately with the environment. Whether or not the Club of Rome and the authors of *The Limits to Growth* have overstated or simplified their case, they nonetheless have pinpointed some serious issues.[14] Unfortunately, the shortcomings in their arguments have provoked severe criticisms which have led some, especially economists, to attempt to discredit the whole issue. At times the arguments of the opponents of *The Limits to Growth* are just as overstated and simplified as those advanced by the proponents.

One of the chief claims of those who oppose *The Limits to Growth* argument is that the Club of Rome and other alarmists fail to acknowledge that when supplies of raw materials become scarce, the economy will begin to ration and preserve those commodities which are in short supply. As Peter Passell, Marc Roberts, and Leonard Ross see it, "In the real world, rising prices act as an economic signal to conserve scarce resources, providing incentives to use cheaper materials in their place, stimulating research efforts on new ways to save on resource inputs and making renewed exploration attempts more profitable."[15] Once set into motion, such actions supposedly should make it highly unlikely that the planet will ever run short of raw materials. And in the kind of circular reasoning of which economists are so fond, Passell, Roberts, and Ross conclude that, so far, all is well because "in fact natural resource prices have remained low, giving little evidence of coming shortages."

What is less than comforting about such arguments is that the traditional economic analysis used by these critics is not equipped to deal with the kinds of issues that today's ecologists are raising. On balance, economic theory and practice works reasonably well with day-to-day problems and, if need be, with those of a generation or so ahead or behind. But neither economists nor other social scientists are accustomed to dealing in terms of centuries or millennia. Yet that is the time reference we must use when we consider ecological matters and natural resources.

The first thing to note is that the discount mechanism and present value calculations that economists normally use have no meaning when the time span covers centuries or longer periods of time. Even if we discount the future at a very low interest rate, the mechanism of compound interest tends to reduce to quite insignificant amounts the current value of something that will have value only 100 or 1,000 years hence. There is simply no way that the economic system can take account of the fact that it took our planet $4\frac{1}{2}$ billion years to reach its present state.

As we saw, another factor holding down the price of raw materials is that most owners of resource deposits, particularly those in the less developed countries, are much more interested in the present than they are in the future. No matter how attractive a calculation may be which shows that a country's oil will be worth considerably more 10, 50, 100, or 1,000 years in the future, most of us want to enjoy the royalties now. To the extent that we worry at all about our heirs, we usually console ourselves with the promise that we will use the proceeds from our current resource exploitation to provide for their future. This pressure to sell serves to keep the prices of raw materials low. Collusive or cartel arrangements to control sales in order to force the price up have not been very successful in the past. The recent increase in the price of oil is the result of political pressure as much as anything. Moreover, it would be wishful thinking to suggest that the Middle Eastern countries are being motivated to seek higher prices for their oil in order to curb consumption. The Middle Eastern oil dealers are concerned primarily with increasing their prices in order to increase their profits. The last thing in the world they would want is for their total profits, or even their total revenues, to fall. With a cartel and rising demand, they feel it possible to have both higher prices and higher sales.

Finally, economists, of all people, should be the last ones on earth to expect prices to respond to environmental forces. Economists, more than anyone else, have been bemoaning the failure of all prices to reflect the social costs arising from the production and sale of goods. This is a shortcoming which no economic system has been able to overcome. Given these inadequacies, it is unrealistic to suggest that an increase in prices will provide adequate warning of an impending crisis. By the time prices start to increase, the situation is likely to be already quite severe.

Conclusion

The prospects for a voluntary reduction in economic growth and for an effective program of environmental control are not very bright. Except for the hippie and the commune movement, the urge to increase one's economic well-being continues to pervade our times. Occasionally someone such as the governor of Delaware or Oregon will try to divert some of the more onerous forms of growth by restricting the future expansion of heavy industry in his state, but even such mavericks do not turn their backs on *all* economic growth. Moreover, it frequently turns out that many who do oppose growth (including some in the communes) are those who are already relatively well off.

The striving for more and the determination "to manifest nature" (to dominate and manipulate it to serve our purposes and designs) are not peculiar to rich capitalist societies. In fact, as destructive as capitalism has been to the environment, there is little, except blind faith, to indicate that other economic systems or economics in general have treated or will treat it any better.

Notes

[1] *Newsweek*, June 12, 1972, p. 54.
[2] Barry Commoner, *The Closing Circle* (New York: Alfred A.

Knopf, 1971), p. 281; Boston Museum of Science, *Focus on the Quality of Life* (Boston, 1971), p. 13.

[3] See, for example, Marshall I. Goldman, *The Spoils of Progress: Environmental Pollution in the Soviet Union* (Cambridge: MIT Press, 1972).

[4] K. E. Gabyshev, "Ekonomicheskaia otsenka prirodnykh resursov i rentnye platezhi," *Vestnik Moskovskogo universiteta, seriia ekonomika,* 1969, No. 5, p. 18.

[5] Marshall I. Goldman, "Red Black Gold," *Foreign Policy,* September 1972, p. 138.

[6] *Trud,* November 12, 1966, p. 2; *Izvestia,* February 4, 1967, p. 3; *Pravda,* August 3, 1968, p. 1.

[7] *Literaturnaia gazeta,* May 31, 1972, p. 10; see also *Current Digest of the Soviet Press,* June 28, 1972, p. 31; *Sovetskaia estoniia,* July 7, 1972, p. 3.

[8] United Nations, *The Statistical Yearbook for 1971,* 1972, pp. 10–14.

[9] *The New York Times,* February 13, 1972, p. 11.

[10] Jimoh Omo-Fadaka, "An Alternative to Imperialist Development," *The Ecologist,* June 1972, p. 28.

[11] *Ekonomicheskaia gazeta,* 1968, No. 24, p. 43.

[12] *Wall Street Journal,* June 12, 1972, p. 12.

[13] Jimoh Omo-Fadaka, "Tanzanian Way to Self-Reliance," *The Ecologist,* February 1972, p. 7.

[14] Donella H. Meadows, Dennis L. Meadows, Jorgen Randers, William W. Behrens III, *The Limits to Growth* (New York: Universe Books, 1972).

[15] Peter Passell, Marc Roberts, Leonard Ross, review of *The Limits to Growth* in *The New York Times Book Review,* April 2, 1972, p. 1; see the similar argument by Carl Kaysen, "The Computer That Printed Out W* O* L* F*," *Foreign Affairs,* July 1972, p. 665.

6 | Social consequences of zero economic growth

LINCOLN H. DAY

THE SOCIAL consequences of a zero-growth rate constitute a vast and complex subject. What I intend is to outline an analytical approach for consideration of the topic and follow this with some specific examples of the social consequences most likely to emanate from a condition of zero economic growth. I am not going to discuss how zero economic growth might be either brought about or retained;[1] my focus here will be on the consequences.*

Basic premises

Let me begin with some basic premises which are sometimes overlooked. First, I think we can all accept as a minimum goal a good standard of health and decency for all of mankind, obtained at a minimum psychological and social cost and with minimum deleterious consequences for the environment. Among some of the world's peoples, the attainment of this goal would mean a lower material level of living; among others, a higher material level of living.

---

* The views and opinions expressed in this paper are those of the author and do not necessarily reflect those of the United Nations.

Second, it should be fairly obvious that not everything worthwhile may be obtained in the marketplace. Friendship, health, happiness, intellectual stimulation, beauty, the respect of one's peers, a sense of community, all these and more are measured by no economic indicator and, consequently, figure not at all in the calculation of Gross National Product. Economic goals are but intermediate goals to the attainment of these truly basic ends, and the suitability of economic goals ought to be judged accordingly.

The third basic premise is that many worthwhile things that *can* be measured in economic terms are either already provided in ways that make no demand on nonrenewable resources, or conceivably could be. I would put most educational services in this category, along with most health services; art, literature, music, and drama; housing; outdoor recreation; and a variety of services such as social work, counseling, family planning, probation and parole, and judicial review.

The fourth premise is that many other worthwhile things that can be measured in economic terms and that do require nonrenewable resources could (with a little incentive and effort) be provided not only in ways that would lessen the rate at which nonrenewable resources are used, but also in ways that would involve less harmful effects for the environment. There are a variety of means to this end. They include a more efficient use of materials in manufacture; the use of better varieties of seed and livestock; the application of practices more conducive to the conservation of land and water; better storage practices; and the recycling of metals and other materials, as was accomplished on such a wide scale on the home front during World War II.

Transportation offers particularly wide-ranging possibilities on this score. Just think of what could be gained for both the environment and the quality of life if we stopped building roads and eliminated the private automobile as a means of mass transit. Or, on a lesser scale, think of the reduction in noise pollution that would come from a curfew on aircraft landings and takeoffs during the hours when most people are trying to sleep—something now in effect in both Australia and Washington, D. C. The control of insects through greater variety in land use and crop planning instead of pesticides is another example. Still another is the prohibition of non-returnable or non-biodegradable containers for food and drink, and of plastics and metal foils for packaging.

As for those worthwhile things that *do* require nonrenewable resources, there would seem to be a number of possibilities for improvements in quality and efficiency that would actually result in a *lower* rate of economic growth than that now associated with the provision of these goods and services. The substitution of mass transit systems for private automobiles, and of nondisposable containers for disposable ones, are two examples.

I take it, therefore, that when we proclaim the desirability—or even the necessity—for a zero economic-growth rate, what we have in mind is zero economic growth insofar as the use of nonrenewable resources is concerned. The possible *moral* gains from Spartan simplicity I shall leave to the discussion of others. Economic growth in certain areas is still possible without additional consumption of nonrenewable resources; such growth is still desirable, especially with respect to the provision of the basic necessities of life in some of the underdeveloped countries—allowing, of course, for cultural differences. The point is to achieve these particular kinds of growth at the least cost and with the greatest gain in terms of environmental and human well-being. One element of this would obviously be the simultaneous achievement of a cessation of certain other kinds of growth—namely, those that have deleterious social and ecological side effects. But zero economic growth itself is not necessarily to be equated with the absence of economic and social change.

Consequences of zero economic growth

What, then, might be the consequences for human society of a zero economic-growth rate? Let me note four basic considerations to help put the question in proper context.

First, it is often assumed that the consequences of a zero growth rate will be so pervasive that societies with that characteristic will all display an essential sameness. Yet, on the basis of what is known of such societies (e.g., the medieval feudal societies of Europe, nonindustrialized tribal societies studied by anthropologists, and even the world's industrialized societies during much of the present century), it would seem at least possible for zero economic growth to coexist with a considerable variety of social conditions. The nature of these social conditions would seem, in fact, to depend far more on the context in which this zero economic growth occurs—on the political, social, and demographic milieu, for example—than on the condition of zero economic growth itself.

So far as the distribution of wealth is concerned, societies with zero growth rates could conceivably range from a state of considerable equality to one of gross inequality. However, at the international level, equality among different countries would seem highly unlikely. This would also be true of the distribution of power, in large part because of the dependence of power on wealth.

Second, a zero overall economic-growth rate would not seem to preclude the existence of considerable variety in the rates of change for the various sectors of economic and social activity. These different rates of change would have different consequences, of course, depending on the different social and economic conditions in which they obtained.

Third, it is doubtful if zero economic growth could proceed for very long in the face of continued population growth. For population growth to continue simultaneously with zero economic growth, food production would have to account for an ever greater share of total production. The ultimate result would be an economy of the merest subsistence. Particularly if the population could remember having earlier experienced a higher-than-subsistence level, the result of continued population increase in conjunction with a zero economic-growth rate would likely be considerable social unrest. In any case, zero population growth is a desirable goal in itself—and an inevitable eventuality—regardless of the rate of economic growth. Barring mass emigration (assuming there would be someplace to go), there are only two paths to its attainment: higher mortality or lower fertility. Many of the apparent consequences of zero *economic* growth are really ascribable to the effects of zero *population* growth. However, these effects will differ in response to such factors as the existing economic and social system, the size of the population at the point when zero growth is achieved, the degree of dispersion or concentration of population, and whether zero population growth is maintained essentially through low birth rates or high death rates.

Fourth and finally, it is absolutely essential that in discussing the likely consequences of a zero economic-growth rate, we deal separately with industrialized and nonindustrialized societies.

In short, zero economic growth would seem to be possible under a variety of living conditions and social systems; the causal relationships between a zero economic-growth rate and various conditions of life are by no means either very obvious or necessarily very clear-cut or straightforward. In the long run, and probably in the short run as well, a zero economic-growth rate will necessitate a zero or even negative population-growth rate. Finally, the consequences of a zero economic-growth rate in industrialized countries are likely to be significantly different from those in nonindustrialized societies.

Although we can make some probable predictions, there is certainly enough possible variety in the answers to make the question of the social consequences of a zero economic-growth rate an intellectually intriguing one, whatever the practical implications of the answers. Moreover, there is a measure of safety afforded the prophet in the fact that no one is likely to be in a position to check on the accuracy of his prophecies during his lifetime. Not only are the causal relationships very complex, but zero economic growth will, I am afraid, be a long time in coming. It may, in fact, be so long in coming that the resource base it is intended to save will have been affected—even used up—to a degree beyond salvation.

The industrialized countries

Given this pessimistic outlook, what can we say about the likely consequences of a zero economic-growth rate in the industrialized (i.e., "developed") countries? Let us begin with the industrialized countries because the social changes associated with attaining a zero growth rate are likely to be of greater magnitude and social pervasiveness in these countries than in the non-industrialized countries. One should not minimize the emotional difficulties that may be associated with rejection of the growth ethic—in both affluent and nonaffluent societies. The idea that further economic growth will alleviate the problems of the poor in industrialized countries and of society in general in the nonindustrialized ones seems widely held and has been systematically encouraged by a variety of persons and agencies. But the pervasiveness of this idea is probably markedly different between the two sets of societies. Certainly there are marked differences between them in the levels of growth contemplated.

Of the several ways in which the likely consequences of a zero economic-growth rate might be presented, I have chosen here to list them according to four, not altogether separate, general categories of relationship, as follows: social structure, personality traits, interpersonal relations, and conditions of life.

The effect on society's social structure

What effect zero economic growth will have on a society's social structure will essentially depend on the value that society places on equality in the distribution of goods and services, and also on the extent to which there exists in that society an equality of power—power not only over others, but power also over the social forces that affect one's life and well-being. Are Americans and the Swiss, for example, any happier, any "better off" now than in, say, 1950 when their "real" incomes were substantially lower? To improve the lot of people in the affluent countries, do we need more economic growth or do we need instead a more equitable distribution of wealth? It would seem to me that, in the absence of a more equitable *distribution* of wealth, further economic *growth* in these countries would offer little in the way of social benefit—and could actually make matters a good deal worse.

There is no shortage of proponents of further growth, however. A frequently offered argument for continued economic growth is that it permits improvement in the lot of the poor without altering relative social positions. However, as the pie grows larger, the proportionate shares remain the same—and, though seldom mentioned, the discrepancy in gross amounts becomes ever greater. Presidential advisor Daniel P. Moynihan put the initial version of this case succinctly in a report to President Nixon:

> There is every reason to be concerned about the costs of economic growth, and [the] need for a balanced national growth policy. . . . But this is quite a different thing from proclaiming the immediate necessity to put an end to growth. . . . In . . . general terms, how much sense would this make for society, given *the great stabilizing role of economic growth which makes it possible to increase the incomes of less well off groups in the population without having to decrease the incomes of others?* [Italics added.][2]

Though the adherents of this view seem still in the majority among the holders of political and economic power, at least in the United States, I get the impression that the social and ecological cost of policies embodying such a view is becoming increasingly obvious. These include the social and economic cost of the status frustration and money worries these policies entail for the majority whose incomes never quite reach a comfortable level; the basic injustice embodied in the so obvious divorce of reward from merit and of the social return from social contribution; and, in recent years, the fact that such a system of rewards (and, conversely, of punishments) entails so much environmental loss in the form of ever greater consumption of ever scarcer resources on the part of those in the most fa-vored economic positions. As I summarized it in an article published over a dozen years ago:

> No group in . . . society can repay all of the social costs entailed by its excess reproduction — the rich probably least of all, for their style of life requires a much higher consumption of those very things upon which population increase — in whatever class — places a premium: raw materials and space.[3]

An affluent society can take several paths to greater social equality: greater equalization of incomes; distribution of a greater proportion of goods and ser-vices outside the market system (e.g., health and medi-cal care, recreation, retirement benefits, schooling, trans-portation, and housing) ; or limiting what the rich can do with their money (preventing ownership of seashore and lakefront property, and curtailing the use of auto-mobiles, for example).

However, there is no necessary causal relation-ship between zero economic growth and any of these procedures. It is quite possible for an affluent society to have a large proportion of its population at a position two or three rungs above the bottom—and in no mood to make common cause with those below them. This part of the population is quite capable of reacting to zero eco-nomic growth, at least for a while, by endeavoring to distinguish its position even more clearly from that of those deemed its social "inferiors." We see this in the German lower middle class's early receptivity to Nazism[4] and in the United States today, in the union restrictions on minority-group membership and the opposition to busing on behalf of greater educational opportunities for minority-group children. Nor is there any dearth of evidence to demonstrate that, even in a political democ-racy, those at the top of the power structure can be fully capable of manipulating public opinion and voting behavior to their own ends over extended periods of time. Nonetheless, I should expect that zero economic growth would generally be more conducive to social equality than to social inequality, particularly in a political democracy. For one thing, there would be less with which to "buy off" the have-less portion of the population. For another, there would be less need for capital formation on behalf of future growth, and therefore at least the possibility of allocating a greater share of national income to such things as pensions. If this were done, it would cut down considerably on those instances of income inequality—notably in such affluent countries as the United States, the Federal Republic of Germany, and Australia—where the aged occupy a particularly disadvantaged economic position.[5] A further reason is the likelihood of greater equality of wealth as a result of fewer opportunities for rapid advance in position or income as a consequence of stock-market or real-estate speculation, or of association with a rapidly growing industry or production process. Finally, there is the age structure of a stationary population. If mortality levels are reasonably low, such a population will offer little opportunity for promotion before age fifty or fifty-five, except as a consequence of business expansion—which, of course, would be less likely in a zero-growth economy. This could, of course, result for a time in heightened competition (and, consequently, heightened frustration) ; however, eventually one should expect aspirations to conform more closely to actual opportunities, especially if there is little advertising and little general economic expansion.[6]

Another consequence of zero economic growth for the social structure would be the changes in the composition of the work force as a result of the changes in the composition of output. Certainly one element in attaining a zero-growth economy would be the pruning back of industries geared to growth—machine tools and engines, advertising, steel, stock markets, and some types of construction—and a corresponding increase in the service sector: maintenance and repair and various professional and semiprofessional services. An increase in the proportion of the work force employed in agriculture is also likely if there is—as one would expect— a return to more labor-intensive methods; and also improvement in pensions of a sort that would enable more of the aged to remain on (or return to) farms, where they could be at least partially occupied and could also grow some of their own feed and fiber.

As the archetypical industry of the affluent, growth-oriented economy, advertising would, in a no-growth economy, occupy a position of little significance; for the main tasks of advertising—product differentiation and the creation of needs[7]—would be of little importance. For much the same reasons, there should be a decline in the number of salesmen, though not necessarily of salesclerks and shopkeepers, in the numbers engaged in packaging and commercial design, and in those employed with the media of mass communication. The creative energies of those people, now so highly mobilized in furtherance of the growth ethic, will simply have to be applied to activities more in keeping with the human and ecological necessity of no-growth.

As previously stated, there would be an increase in the numbers employed as maintenance and repair workers, as agricultural workers, and in the provision of a great variety of personal and social services—from birth control to homemaking, from tailoring and dressmaking to day care and supervision of parole and probation. It is in the expansion of such services (and the corresponding contraction of manufacturing) that a zero economic-growth rate will have its greatest impact on the occupational structure of the society.

The changes in industrial and occupational composition would contribute to changes in the patterns of settlement as well. Under conditions of zero economic growth, we could expect the population to be less highly urbanized, and the urban portion of the population to be less concentrated in the very large metropolitan centers. (Note that it is *proportions* I am talking about here, not *numbers;* anticipated population increases are unlikely to permit much reduction in the actual numbers living in the already existing large agglomerations.)

Under conditions of zero economic growth, there would be less economic need for large concentrations of workers; and if the forecasted changes in pension systems and agricultural methods take place, there would also be more living on the land. Accompanied by greater general equality in the distribution of income, an increase in the proportion on the land could be a factor in providing the economic base necessary to settlement of a higher proportion of the population in the smaller towns and cities.

What the consequences of a zero economic-growth rate might be for another feature of social structure, the delineation of male and female roles, is a bit difficult to foresee. If there is greater income equality (and particularly if this equality arises more from equality of wages than from progressive taxation), I should expect a less rigid division of occupations into "men's work" and "women's work." On the other hand, because the newer occupations have customarily provided more employment opportunities to women than have the older ones (unless marked by significantly lower pay rates), a slowing down of economic expansion could result in a greater rigidity of job definition according to sex.[8] The effects of this might be compensated for by the expansion of the service sector; however, there is no assurance that rigid categorization according to sex would not occur in the service sector as well.

Personality traits

Let me turn now to consideration of the effect of a zero economic-growth rate on the distribution of personality traits. There are a number of possibilities.

There should be an eventual decline in the emphasis on "getting ahead."[9] The desire for a second job and the readiness to accept overtime work, for example, are features of an economy characterized not so much by abundance as by the unequal distribution of wealth and the anticipation of economic growth.

At the same time, there should be a development of a more positive attitude toward work itself. What is undertaken would presumably be of more obvious use, and also more likely to have developed in response to a *genuine* demand and not merely a *created* one. (There could still be some advertising to create demand for certain goods and services, but, as already noted, advertising and zero economic growth are essentially incompatible.) Moreover, the worker, at least in manufacturing, could be expected to take pride in his product because quality and durability rather than style and obsolescence would have been emphasized in its manufacture.[10] And finally, the individual worker would play a larger role in the total product process and acquire a greater sense of identity with the results of his labors. A zero-growth economy, particularly if combined with a more equal distribution of wealth, would seemingly offer less incentive to substitute machine work for handwork or to apply the more markedly dehumanizing techniques of minute specialization.

In a zero-growth economy, work could come to be considered less as simply a means to an end and more as an end in itself. This would be especially true if the work situation afforded opportunity for creativity and for the development of emotionally satisfying relations with one's associates. Though these opportunities have always characterized many jobs, even in highly industrialized economies, the tendency toward this sort of thing would be considerably enhanced by a lessened emphasis on "efficiency" and specialization in the production process, by a lower level of material aspiration, and by a lessening of competition with one's fellow workers.

Along with these changes in attitudes toward work and toward getting ahead, the members of a zero economic-growth society would probably also be less inept outside their jobs than their counterparts in societies characterized by economic growth.[11] The decline of specialization would be a factor here; so would the greater experience with repairing things instead of throwing them away, and possibly, also, with producing things for oneself—furniture, clothes, toys, and canned goods, for example.

There should be a greater feeling of being able to cope. Part of this would be due to the development of a wider range of skills. It would also arise from the greater stability, the greater predictability, of a zero-growth society, and from the fact that in such a society there would be less likelihood of personal frustration, whether from thwarted ambition or merely commuter traffic jams.

Unless counterbalanced by the pressure of population on resources, the members of a zero-growth society would be less imbued with the man-*versus*-nature attitude that underlies the exploitative growth economy.[12] A zero-growth economy would appear to offer little support for the view that man's duty is to bend nature to his will rather than learning to live with it.

Finally, the person reared in a condition of zero economic growth could be expected to place little emphasis on growth and bigness as desirable in themselves, and also on the desirability of "change" and "newness." Not for them the unquestioned assumption that what is new is naturally better.

Interpersonal relations

In the area of interpersonal relations, I should expect the major consequence of zero economic growth to be a greater sense of community. A number of factors would contribute. Because private means would be in shorter supply and so much more expensive, we could expect a greater sharing of equipment—from lawn mowers and washing machines to farm machinery and public transportation—with all the possibilities this would offer for informal, psychically rewarding interpersonal contact. There is much more potential for the development of community in doing the wash in a laundromat than in doing it in the basement.[13] Another factor would be the informal mixing of different age groups and social classes which would derive from such sharing, particularly of public transportation. As A. E. Parr has pointed out, it is much more difficult to think of someone as alien, of a different species to be feared or even despised, if you see him every day on the bus.[14] And as Edward T. Hall has written:

> Automobiles insulate man not only from the environment but from human contact as well. They permit only the most limited types of interaction, usually competitive, aggressive, and destructive. If people are to be brought together again, given a chance to get acquainted with each other and involved in nature, some fundamental solutions must be found to the problems posed by the automobile.[15]

Today, eight out of ten American workers go to work in a private automobile—and for three-fourths of them it's a case of one whole automobile encapsulating but one rugged individualist behind the wheel.[16] Little chance, there, for human contact—even of a merely visual sort.

A greater sense of community would also be stimulated by more labor-intensive work processes and a lesser degree of specialization, both of which would be at least partially supported by the need to share equipment. It would also follow from the lesser emphasis on individual competition that would be a likely consequence of zero economic growth. There might still be ample room for competition in the development of invidious distinctions of status (like those so frequently observed in anthropological studies),[17] but in a condition of no-growth such distinctions would necessarily extend over a much narrower range.

Finally, a greater sense of community should arise because a zero economic-growth rate would produce less individual mobility—both social and geographic—and also less community change, particularly of the type forced upon an area by speculative investment and road-building. With less economic development and less speculation, people could be expected to remain longer in their communities and individual places of residence. They would thus have at least the opportunity to develop greater loyalty to the community and a greater sense of identity with it. And, of course, there would be much less incentive to think of home ownership as nothing but a speculative investment.

Less crime and delinquency would occur under conditions of zero economic growth. Affluence has frequently led to the loss of familiar ways and surroundings and to the creation of artificial distinctions within society and of higher aspirations productive of nothing but individual frustration. Without going into the theory of the causation of crime and delinquency, I should expect that anything that resulted in a greater sense of community, more predictability, less advertising, and more demonstrably worthwhile work would result in markedly less crime and delinquency.

For much the same reasons, we might forecast less industrial strife in a no-growth economy, though we must recognize that it is not necessary to have equality of social power in order to have stability of social relationships. There is nothing inherently unstable about social inequality.

Finally, as far as interpersonal relations are concerned, zero economic growth should lead to less conflict between generations: because there would be less change and therefore more predictability and continuity; because there would be more sharing of activities among the generations and more joint participation in the life of the society; and because there would be less advertising and less commercially oriented programming in the media of mass communications to create alternative, age-specific "life styles."

Conditions of life

With respect to conditions of life, it is possible to note a large number of likely changes that would attend achievement of a zero economic-growth rate.

We can expect, for one thing, a substantial change in patterns of work: a shift to shorter work days, to part-time work, or to working only part of the year; none of these need necessarily mean more leisure, however, as the time saved from work could, of course, be merely transferred to lengthier commuting.

Yet it is possible that the time spent on the job could remain much the same because the lower total output necessary to zero economic growth would be attained through the use of "less productive" methods, such as substituting labor for capital and reducing the stress on minute specialization.

One would forecast more emphasis on preservation and conservation, whether of land or old buildings, although population pressure may reach such extremes in some countries as to prevent any real halt in the drift to total environmental decay.

In some sectors of the economy, zero growth would reduce consumer choice in clothing, food, and consumer durables. But in others, such as recreation and the availability of public transportation, a zero-growth economy might offer a wider choice.

Even with the development of solar and tidal sources of energy, a zero-growth economy would, by definition, involve a lower consumption of energy—industrially and commercially, and also within individual households. At the level of daily living, this would take such forms as the disappearance of the private automobile, the heating of water only for immediate use, less central heating, and less air conditioning.

Despite such inconveniences, I should expect life in a zero-growth economy to be generally more comfortable than it is now.

Along with other factors already mentioned, there would be less air and water pollution, and less waste disposal, although population increases could in both instances cancel the gains inherent in zero economic growth. There should be considerably less noise pollution because there would be fewer cars and airplanes and fewer trucks hauling cargoes of disposable obsolete goods. Public transportation would be more prominent and traffic jams less. With less forced obsolescence, with a greater emphasis on durability in manufacturing and on ease of repair, and with a larger proportion of the work force engaged in repair and maintenance, there would be fewer breakdowns of equipment and less waiting for repairs. And there would be more possibilities for an attractive environment—the result of less advertising, fewer motor vehicles, less need for rapid construction (because population would have ceased to increase, and a zero rate of economic growth would require less internal migration), and less incentive to destroy the old to make way for the new. A return to "less efficient" methods of production might well have as one of its first consequences a decided improvement in the aesthetic quality of houses and buildings.

The nonindustrialized countries

Now let me turn briefly to the nonindustrialized countries. Zero economic growth here would involve much less extensive or pervasive changes. Most of these countries are not presently far removed from zero economic growth. Were they to attain it now, they would do so at a largely subsistence level. However, in some instances this level of living has approached the idyllic. Here, for example, is Frances FitzGerald's description of conditions in prewar Vietnam villages:

> For traditional Vietnamese, the sense of limitation and enclosure was a part of individual life as much as the life of the nation. In what is today northern and central Vietnam, the single form of Vietnamese settlement duplicated the closed circle of the nation. Hidden from sight behind high hedges of bamboo, the villages stood like nuclei within their encircling rice fields. For the villages, as for the nation, the amount of arable land was absolutely inelastic. The population of the village remained stable, and so to accumulate wealth was to deprive the rest of the community of land, to fatten while one's neighbor starved. Vietnam is no longer a closed economic system, but the idea remains with many Vietnamese that great wealth is anti-social — not a sign of success but a sign of selfishness.
> With a stable technology and a limited amount of land,

the traditional Vietnamese lived by constant repetition, by the sowing and reaping of rice and by the perpetuation of customary law. . . . In this passage of time that had no history, the death of a man marked no real end. Buried in the rice fields that sustained his family, the father would live on in the bodies of his children and grand-children. As time wrapped around itself, the generations to come would regard him as the source of their present lives and the arbiter of their fate. In this continuum of the family, "private property" did not really exist, for the father was less an owner than a trustee of the land to be passed on to his children. To the Vietnamese, the land itself was the sacred, constant element: the people flowed over the land like water, maintaining and fructifying it for the generations to come.[18]

Unfortunately, such conditions are fast disappearing in the face of contact with other cultures and of rapid population increases. Elsewhere in the nonindustrialized world, life may be more appropriately characterized as "nasty, brutish, and short." Few of these societies can, as yet, really afford zero economic growth —if only because of political considerations. By almost any criterion, most of them offer much room for improvement in living conditions; "improvement" presumably in terms of their own cultures and aspirations, and not just in terms of some Western viewpoint. They are in need of better nutrition, health care, birth control, and housing; and in many instances, also, of jobs and of more opportunities for people to play a meaningful role in society.

Quite apart from any considerations either of justice or of the politics inherent in the enormous discrepancies in levels of living that separate the industrialized from the nonindustrialized lands, most of the latter will require massive assistance from the former, if only to hold the line against further depredations. In general, these countries lack the social base (e.g., in schooling and productive agriculture) necessary for economic development and are, in most instances, further disadvantaged by a youthful age structure and rapid rates of population increase.

Essentially, the achievement of zero economic growth in these currently nonindustrialized countries would preclude their ever becoming industrialized. With a goal of zero economic growth, their efforts to increase productivity would presumably be channeled into the production of food and services, rather than into activities that would yield revenue for the purchase of goods manufactured from nonrenewable resources.

There is at least a theoretical opportunity for these countries to grow because they have, for the most part, proceeded such a short way along the road to industrialization. But this would seem, in most cases, to be more than outweighed by a number of other attributes. Most of the nonindustrialized countries have but limited resources, even if the goal of development is merely of a strictly nonindustrial sort. Moreover, many have large populations, and all are experiencing rapid population increases—with no migratory outlets and every indication that these increases will continue many decades into the future. And thus far these countries give little evidence of experiencing social changes of a sort conducive to attainment of a reduction in fertility levels commensurate with the need to halt population increase. There is a very practical question here: Given the desirability of better health and greater longevity (and thus of lower mortality rates), how much—and what kind of—social change is necessary to produce a willingness to limit family size to the degree necessary to keep this low-mortality population stationary? Is industrialization now a requisite? We have some clues, even if we don't know the answer for certain; it takes only a look at the statistics to see that, whatever the necessary changes, they are not occurring fast enough to forestall continuing massive population increases many years into the future. Yet the prospect for any improvement in living conditions hinges very significantly upon when, how, and at what numerical levels the nonindustrialized countries finally succeed in reducing the birthrates to the levels of the death rates.

Conclusion

A zero economic-growth rate offers the possibility of a better life in the currently industrialized countries; and certainly conditions in these countries have already reached a point beyond which the possibilities for improvement by means of further economic growth are virtually nil. For the nonindustrialized countries, however, there is less certainty about this—except, of course, in the long run. Any decline in the extent of the dualism that separates the rich from the poor, both among nations and within them, is to be applauded.[19] But large international differences in living conditions will doubtless remain. Will this be a source of frustration and, therefore, of social and political disruption in the less industrialized countries? With communication as developed as it now is, this kind of frustration can hardly be avoided; nevertheless, it need not lead inevitably to social disorder. Any reduction in the living-standard gap would probably help, especially if in the nonindustrialized countries this were accomplished in ways that left the basic elements of their cultures relatively intact as a cushion to fall back on, while in the more affluent countries it involved an actual reduction in material levels of living.

Differences in international power are bound to continue. The attainment of zero economic growth will help to reduce these differences, but there will always be the possibility that the leaders of countries with more power will be able to divert economic and social processes within these countries away from maintenance of zero economic growth and into economic growth on behalf of some military adventure instead. We will thus continue to need international organizations for the settlement of differences and for the keeping of the peace, whatever the likely economic situation. However, the task of such organizations might be far easier under conditions of zero economic growth. There would be less social and economic room for maneuver on behalf of military action, and it would be far more difficult for a government to divert its people's dislike of a policy of military aggrandizement and carnage by appealing to their fears about losses of jobs or cuts in personal income.

Notes

[1] In this connection, see Kenneth E. Boulding, "The Economics of the Coming Spaceship Earth," in Henry Jarrett (ed.), *Environmental Quality in a Growing Economy* (Baltimore: Johns Hopkins University Press, 1966). Also see the following sophisticated and broad-gauged discussions by Herman E. Daly: "Toward a Stationary-State Economy," in John Harte and Robert H. Socolow (eds.), *Patient Earth* (New York: Holt, Rinehart & Winston, 1971); "The Stationary-State Economy," *The Ecologist*, July 1972; and "On the Transition to a Steady-State Economy," in Herman E. Daly (ed.), *Toward a Steady-State Economy* (San Francisco: W. H. Freeman, 1972) (forthcoming).

[2] Daniel P. Moynihan, "Counsellor's Statement," in National Goals Research Staff, *Toward Balanced Growth: Quantity and Quality* (Washington: U.S. Government Printing Office, 1970), p. 12.

[3] Lincoln H. Day, "The American Fertility Cult," *Columbia*

University Forum, Summer 1960.

[4] Hans Gerth, "The Nazi Party: Its Leadership and Composition," *American Journal of Sociology*, January 1940; Franz Neumann, *Behemoth: The Structure and Practice of National Socialism* (New York: Oxford University Press, 1942).

[5] U.S. Department of Health, Education, and Welfare, Social Security Administration, Office of Research and Statistics, Research Report No. 40, *Social Security Programs throughout the World, 1971* (Washington: U.S. Government Printing Office, 1972); A. J. Jaffe, "Retirement: A Cloudy Future," *Industrial Gerontology*, Summer 1972, Chap. 5; Michael Harrington, *The Other America* (New York: Macmillan, 1963), Chap. 6; "Have-nots of the 'Economic Miracle,' " *London Times*, July 21, 1972.

[6] Lincoln H. Day, "The Social Consequences of a Zero Population Growth Rate in the United States," in U.S. Commission on Population Growth and the American Future, *Report* (Washington: U.S. Government Printing Office, 1972) (forthcoming).

[7] David M. Potter, *People of Plenty* (Chicago: University of Chicago Press, 1954), Chap. 8.

[8] Theodore Caplow, *The Sociology of Work* (Minneapolis: University of Minnesota Press, 1954), Chap. 10.

[9] See in this connection, A. J. Jaffe, "Retirement: A Cloudy Future," *op. cit.*, pp. 76–77, and also A. J. Jaffe, *The Middle Years: Neither Too Young Nor Too Old*, special issue of *Industrial Gerontology*, September 1971, Chap. 10.

[10] Paul Goodman, *Growing Up Absurd* (New York: Random House, 1960), pp. 17–22.

[11] *Ibid.*, pp. 71–79.

[12] Kenneth Boulding, *op. cit.*

[13] See, for example, "Launderettes," *Which?*, July 1967 (published by the Consumers Association, United Kingdom).

[14] A. E. Parr, "Urbanity and the Urban Scene," *Landscape*, Spring 1967.

[15] Edward T. Hall, *The Hidden Dimension* (Garden City, New York: Doubleday, 1966), p. 177.

[16] *New York Times* (report on the 1970 census), October 15, 1972.

[17] James West, *Plainville, U.S.A.* (New York: Columbia University Press, 1945), Chap. 3; Allison Davis, Burleigh B.

Gardner, and Mary R. Gardner, *Deep South* (Chicago: University of Chicago Press, 1941), Chaps. 3 and 10.

[18] Frances FitzGerald, "Fire in the Lake," Part I, *New Yorker*, July 1, 1972, p. 38.

[19] United Nations, Department of Economic and Social Affairs, *1970 Report on the World Social Situation* (New York, 1971), pp. xi and 66 (Table 12)).

7 | Zero economic growth and the distribution of income

LESTER THUROW

EARLIER IN THESE sessions, geological time was made comprehensible to our finite human minds by the statement that the 4½ billion years of earth's history was equivalent to once around the world in an SST. If I remember the numbers correctly, man got on eight miles before the end, and industrial man got on six feet before the end. The participants in this symposium all got on some fraction of a millimeter before the end, and today we are having a debate about the extent to which man ought to maximize the length of time that he is on that airplane.

According to what the scientists now think, the sun is gradually expanding, and 12 billion years from now the earth will be swallowed up by the sun. That means that our airplane has time to go around the world three more times. Do we want man to be on it for all three times around the world? Are we interested in man being on for another eight miles? Are we interested in man being on for another six feet? Or are we only interested in man for a fraction of a millimeter—our lifetime?

Earlier Simon Rottenberg was asking Marshall Goldman to give him a discount rate. Marshall Goldman said, "Well, I'm convinced that the market rate of interest is *not* the right discount rate because it doesn't consider what's going to happen a thousand years from now." That led me to think: Do I care what happens a thousand years from now? Do I care when man gets off the airplane? And I think I basically came to the conclusion that I don't care whether man is on the airplane for another eight feet, or if man is on the airplane another three times around the earth.

The problem is similar to that of abortion. Do you believe it is appropriate for women to abort children or use birth control? Do you believe it is appropriate for this generation to abort a future generation? We have a group in Massachusetts that is fighting abortion bills. It is called "The Right to Life Group," and it has introduced a very peculiar bill into the state legislature. The bill implies that you have committed murder anytime there is an unfertilized egg. When does life begin? At what level am I worried about it? Well, I am willing to let any woman abort any child, and if you came to me and said, "Look, I know that all women of the world are going to abort all children so that we will abort the next generation," would I then make it illegal to have abortions? My answer is no. If people around the world want to abort the next generation, I don't regard that as something that I ought to be worrying about. We can have different moral values. You may say, "I am interested in how long man is on that airplane. I want him to be on that airplane for the next three times around the world. Therefore I have a very high negative discount rate." That may be a reasonable view. I do think it really comes down to a value judgment—how long you think man ought to be on the airplane as it goes around the world for its three missions. I myself come down on the side of the relatively high positive discount rate which minimizes the value of the distant future.

When we are discounting the future, there are

two things we must consider. We have to figure out our time rate of discount, *and* we have to figure out the uncertainty premium we want to add to that pure time rate of discount. My pure time rate of discount is 5 or 6 percent or higher—reasonably high. My uncertainty premium is at least another 5 or 6 percent. Now let's take that generation in existence a thousand years from now. What could I best do *now* that would help it? I confess to not knowing the answer. Would it be that I shouldn't use any oil? These people are going to be desperate for oil a thousand years from now. But an equally plausible scenario is that they are going to have enormous quantities of nuclear wastes, and the best thing I could do is dig deep holes in the ground and pump everything out so they have a place to pump things down. I don't know which is right. And I don't think anyone knows which is right. There is some fundamental level of uncertainty in our system. What is our uncertainty premium? My uncertainty premium may be higher than my pure time rate of discount. Looking at the current world, I am not really going to worry about a generation one thousand years from now. It's not yet alive! It is basically equivalent to worrying about my grandparents who are dead. Perhaps under some rubric I can help them. If I were a Mormon, I could go off and get them baptized by proxy and that would help get them out of hell. If I believed in purgatory, I could offer some prayers and that would speed them to heaven. Under some rubric I could help the dead. Under my rubric I don't believe there is anything I could do to help my grandparents who are dead, and I really don't believe there is much I can do, positive or negative, that is going to help a generation one thousand years from now. So I take a more plebeian view of the problem. And it is the more plebeian view that I am going to express here.

I would like to look at periods of negative or

zero economic growth and see what happens. Human history actually has lots of periods of negative and zero growth. From 1929 to 1939 we had negative growth. In 1949, 1954, 1957, 1958, 1960 and 1961 there was zero growth. In 1969-1971 there was zero growth. Fortunately, we don't have any periods in American history with generation after generation of negative growth. If you study American economic history, you can only study the short-run results of a period of zero or negative growth.

However, there are cases in the world where you can analyze the effects of long-run negative rates of growth. I recently spent some time on the Indian subcontinent. I was intrigued. When I came back I began asking my archeological, economic development, and anthropological friends the following question: "Are the current per capita economic standards of living in Bangladesh higher or lower than those of our ancestors when they were living in caves?" Many of my friends speculate that the current economic standards in Bangladesh are probably lower than those of our ancestors when they were back in the caves eating each other, presuming you measure living standards by calories consumed, how close you are to subsistence, and life expectancy. It's just not at all obvious that East Bengal has had any economic progress. If you were an expert on Indian economics and culture, you might be able to find a period of long-run negative growth; this would enable you to study long-run negative growth. I don't happen to be enough of an expert to do that; I am going to confine myself to the short-run American experience, to the transition phase, of negative growth.

What does our study of past periods of negative growth tell us of the problems that emerge? What will we have to do in such periods? Moreover, if we are to study the effects of a "no-growth" economy, we must take the notion of "no-growth" seriously. If we opt for no-growth, we can't weasel out and allow this sector or that to keep growing on the basis that these are not polluting our resource-using sectors.

Ann Carter and the other people who work on the Leontief input-output project are trying to set up disaggregated input-output tables that have resource-using and producing columns. These tables show the direct as well as the indirect pollution effects of various types of activities: leisure activities, service activities, goods-producing activities, etc. When you do that it is hard to come to the standard conclusion that the production of some goods leads to pollution while that of others, like services or education, does not. When both direct and indirect pollution effects are included, almost all activities involve some pollution. Thus, while it's quite true that services don't pollute directly, they generate a lot of indirect pollution. The same thing is true for leisure activities. Take one of my favorite leisure activities—skiing. It takes an airplane to get me to Colorado to go skiing, which creates a great deal of pollution. Take education. Who is the largest consumer of electricity in the Boston area? MIT. Who is the second largest consumer of electricity in the Boston area? The affiliated hospitals of Harvard. It's not at all obvious that we can have lots of health care and lots of education and still not have pollution or use of resources. It may be that when we add the direct and indirect aspects of these activities, they are, in fact, great polluters. In contrast there may be some material goods manufacturers who don't use many resources and don't do much polluting. Until hard information is developed on who pollutes and who doesn't, who uses resources and who doesn't, no-growth should mean no-growth for everyone.

Now suppose we turn back to the econometric studies, the economic history, of periods of zero or negative growth. What happens to the distribution of income in these periods? As we have indicated, the results do not show what will happen in a long-run period of zero economic growth; however, we have some evidence of the problems that would emerge if you simply stopped the merry-go-round. What would you have to change to prevent these problems from emerging?

To approach these problems let us take a counterview and project what will happen if we keep the merry-go-round turning. If we continue to pursue economic growth, the big unknown in the distribution of income depends on what happens in the area of female liberation. In the postwar period we have had a rather constant distribution of family income, measured in relative terms between rich and poor; however, this statistical result was basically produced in spite of widening dispersion of income among adult males by wives going to work in an offsetting fashion. Family-income dispersion was relatively stable because the higher your income, the lower the probability of your having a wife in the labor force. For example, back in 1969 (the last available data), if you earned between $6,000 and $7,000, there was a 49 percent probability that your wife was in the labor force; if you earned over $25,000, the probability of your wife's being in the labor force was only 19 percent. However, if males who earn high incomes are married to women who could earn high incomes in a perfectly fair and liberated world, then women's liberation will make the distribution of family income more unequal. Most of the poor women have already gone to work, and most of the wealthy women have yet to go to work. What happens to the distribution of income in a growing economy depends heavily on the course of women's liberation. Women's liberation makes male-female differentials more equal, but women's liberation is going to make family incomes a lot less equal.

Using econometric techniques, you can determine what happens to income in a recessionary, or zero-growth, period. I am assuming that we really prohibit economic growth by stopping people from working. However, technical progress will continue to occur. If people choose to invest, investment will continue to occur. We enter a zero-growth world by stopping employment through macroeconomic policies, by employing fiscal and monetary policies to produce a zero rate of aggregate growth. The first thing that will occur is rising unemployment. If we shared unemployment equally across the population, then the resulting rise in leisure from 4 percent to 6 percent might not be terribly important. On the other hand, if we share unemployment unequally, so that when unemployment goes from 4 percent to 6 percent, 6 percent of the population is unemployed throughout the year, that would be something very different. Unfortunately the real world is likely to come closer to the latter picture than the former. It is clear from our experience with slowed-down economies that in a zero-growth world we will have to ration jobs.

Now, the current economic system does ration jobs in a recession, but in doing so, it makes the distribution of income much more unequal. At the 25th and 75th percentiles of the income distribution during periods of zero economic growth, the relative gap between those two percentiles increases about 0.2 percent per year among whites; among blacks it increases about 2.3 percent per year. The income dispersion among whites gradually becomes more unequal; the income dispersion among blacks also becomes more unequal, but at a much faster rate. Moreover, black incomes fall relative to white by about 6.5 percent a year for every year of no-growth because the blacks bear a more than proportionate burden of unemployment under our current rationing system. I would not care to argue that you can multiply these numbers by one hundred and describe what conditions would be like a hundred years from now. All that the data show is that our present structure produces a more unequal distribution of the income when you turn off the economy. If you do want to turn off the economy, you must think about a different job-rationing system than the one we now have.

The male-versus-female income problem would also be intensified in a zero-growth population economy. (I define a growth-population economy not as one with a fertility rate of 2.1 children per family, but as a population stabilized at 210 million people, or a fertility rate of 1.2 children per family.) In a women's liberation world, the labor force would grow by 30 percent, even if no additional persons entered our economy. If we turned growth off, there would be no way to liberate women without unliberating men. The whole process of how to ration jobs between males and females becomes a much more difficult problem in a zero-growth world. Economic growth would not equalize black and white income differentials, nor would it equalize the differential between rich and poor. I believe the opposite. However, the one thing economic growth will do is provide more opportunities for women. For a whole variety of reasons, economic growth can provide equal income opportunities between women and men.

However, when you turn off the world, there are some countervailing gains. You can avoid some educational expenditures, and you can avoid some investment expenditures. In a zero-growth population world—1.2 children per family—I figure that the combined savings from reduced education and investment expenditures could raise our real living standards by about 11 percent. In other words, we presently devote about 11 percent of our resources to educating people whom we wouldn't need to educate or to investing in some kind of capital that we wouldn't need. There would be extra resources released in the system from zero growth. On the other hand, you would have some costs. If you shared work more than we do now, that would mean extra training costs. If everyone retired at forty-five, you would need to train people twice as often. I don't know exactly what these training costs would be, but they could actually eat up that 11 percent of net gain.

The income split between young and old depends on how jobs are rationed. In recessionary periods under the current system, if the elderly retain their jobs, their income rises relative to the general population. However, if an elderly person happens to be so unlucky as to become unemployed, he finds it terribly difficult to get re-employed. Nevertheless, since the former effect dominates the latter effect, elderly incomes rise on the average in recessions. Still, there is that group of elderly people that *is* severely handicapped during zero-growth periods.

Income opportunities for the young currently consist of two possibilities: (1) waiting for someone to die, or (2) taking advantage of economic growth to obtain a net new job. In a zero-growth world, somebody must die or retire in order for someone else to get promoted. Bob Solow and I are at the same institution, and we have a reasonably cordial relationship. But I suspect that if I were waiting for Bob Solow to die so I could become a professor of economics, our relationship would not be the same. One of the nice things about economic growth at MIT is that I could become a professor without Bob Solow's dying.

We also need to think a little more seriously about the nature of jobs, as opposed to income. If the only return from a job is income, then the problem is theoretically easily solved. We simply set up a redistribution scheme for income. Nevertheless, having participated in presidential campaigns, I am convinced that income redistribution is very difficult in the real world. A lot of people talk about income redistribution but get frightened when somebody actually proposes it seriously.

There are a lot of people, however, who are currently reassessing their income-redistribution goals. When I give talks on income-redistribution problems, I usually run an interesting experiment. I ask people a variety of questions about America, including what they think the average family income is. One of the questions I ask them to answer anonymously is: "What is your family income, and into what percentile do you think you fall in the income distribution?" I have done this with Wall Street groups, where the average family income was $150,000, and I have done it with poverty groups where the average family income was $3,000. It doesn't make any difference whether you're rich or poor; you will tell me, on average, that you fall between the 40th and 60th percentile. Americans don't want to face up to the fact that they are rich or poor. The problem with actually proposing income redistribution arises when people learn that anybody who earns over $25,000 is in the top half of 1 percent of the income recipients. Everybody thinks that somebody else (the Rockefellers or Howard Hughes or whoever) is rich and that he is poor. I suspect that if you put Getty, Rockefeller, and Hughes in a room and gave them the test, they would say that they fall between the 40th and 60th percentile. It's funny, but it's absolutely true. Everybody is middle class when it comes to putting down his income.

But getting back to the distinction between jobs and income, it is terribly important to become concerned about the nonmarket aspects of jobs. There are a whole host of consumption benefits that flow from jobs that have little to do with money income. I'm standing here having fun talking to you because of my job as professor. There are lots of nonpecuniary benefits that arise from work. You make your friends there. You get status, fame, fortune, power, and so on. The income-distribution problem may be theoretically trivial. How are you going to redistribute the other rewards of society? In the zero-growth world, there are going to be very hard rationing problems with respect to these nonpecuniary goods.

There is a need to be concerned about the nature of markets in a zero-growth world. From my study of economics, I couldn't predict whether markets would become more or less competitive. Imagine a world where a larger proportion of the citizens are elderly and have relatively fixed consumption patterns, where incomes don't rise and, given fixed habit formation, we don't buy as many new things, and where most of us are customers of existing firms. I can imagine a scenario where we would be much less competitive, but I can also imagine a scenario where we would be at each other's throats. What are currently our most competitive activities? They are artificial games, like soccer. Soccer is a zero-sum game. Somebody must win, somebody lose. The emotions are very intense. That's a zero-sum game. The economic system is not a zero-sum game. When I win, you don't have to lose. Basically, we don't tear each other apart quite as badly in economic life as we do in soccer. Whether zero growth would make markets more or less competitive may be a psychoanalytic problem.

There is one other period of economic history worth looking at. In the Great Depression, the other period of negative growth, there were some different results. I have argued that in a recession, quite clearly, the distribution of income becomes more unequal. It is interesting that in the Great Depression the opposite happened: the distribution of income became more equal. Let me cite just a few figures. During the Great

Depression the income share of the bottom 40 percent of the population rose from 12.5 to 13.6 percent. The top 5 percent of the population saw their share of total income fall from 30 to 24 percent, and the share of the top 20 percent of the population fell from 54.4 to 48.8 percent. Thus a noticeably more equal distribution of income was produced by collapsing the economy. There did seem to be some kind of subsistence floor to wages. High wages fell faster than low wages. Capital earnings, a big portion of high incomes, fell much faster than wages. Thus the whole distribution of income became relatively more equal. Perhaps zero economic growth creates a more unequal distribution of income, but perhaps a really substantial negative rate of growth would produce a more equal distribution of income because the process would collapse the current structure. In a collapse, those who have more to lose will lose more than those who have less to lose.

There are actually two periods in our recent economic history in which the distribution of income became more equal: one was the Great Depression, with a high negative rate of growth; the other was World War II, with a very high positive rate of growth. We came out of the Great Depression with the bottom 40 percent of the population having 13.6 percent of the income; during World War II, their share increased to 16 percent and was maintained afterwards. The war started with the top 5 percent having a 24 percent income share, and at the end of the war it was 20.9 percent. The top 20 percent of the population started with a 48.8 percent income share and went down to 46.0 percent. During World War II the mechanism for equalizing incomes did not consist of collapsing the economy, nor was it zero economic growth. The government simply thought that, since people were sacrificing their lives, we ought to have a relatively equal wage structure at home, and it imposed a relatively equal wage structure on the economy. The interesting thing is that this structure was maintained after the war.

Perhaps this points out that if you really want equality, you can have it, whether you are for or against zero economic growth—if you are willing to take some action. My basic hypothesis is that, given the effects of women's liberation, both growth and no-growth will lead to a more unequal distribution of income. If there is a desire for a more equal distribution of income, then some positive redistribution policies are necessary, regardless of whether you are for zero economic growth or for a positive level of economic growth.

8 | Is there an optimum level of population?

S. FRED SINGER

IT MAY SEEM intuitively obvious that a country should have an optimum population level: i.e., the citizens of the country would be better off at this level of population than if the population were less or if it were greater. But intuition can be misleading; therefore, a more careful analysis is needed.

My interest in population problems developed through a progression of positions with the Department of the Interior, the Environmental Protection Agency, and the Brookings Institution. A concern with natural resources and environmental problems led me to study the following questions: What factors provide a limit to population growth? Fuel resources and energy, mineral resources, food, water, or simply land? What will we run out of first? What factors determine the population-carrying capacity of the world—or of the United States? *All* of these factors are involved to a greater or lesser extent.

But perhaps the original question was misleading; it confused the maximum level of population with

ACKNOWLEDGMENTS: I appreciate the assistance of Messrs. Harry Burt, Giorgio Canarella, and James Morris. The research was supported by the Center of Population Research, National Institutes of Health, under contract NIH-NICHD-72-2052.

the optimum. The confusion between the two persists for many; however, the general rule is that the optimum is always less than the maximum.

The optimum population depends not only on the number of people but also on the spatial distribution, on the rate of growth of population, on technological progress, and on a wide variety of parameters which enter into demography and economics. Moreover, the optimum population level is not fixed over time; possibly it decreases with time.

To address the problem of optimum population, one has to develop a method which is much broader than those used to measure carrying capacity and which can answer many other questions. The goals may be rephrased as follows:

What methods can be developed to assess the general societal consequences of governmental policies, of major technological advances, and of private decisions, such as a reduction in fertility, on both the population level and its optimum size? In particular, how can we determine an optimum level of population for a country? This essay gives a progress report on our efforts to develop such methods.

Scope of the study

Our study deals with a projection of the United States over the next thirty to fifty years. The justification for neglecting the rest of the world at this stage is as follows: First, we are interested in methodology, and for this purpose the United States presents a sufficiently complex case. Second, this is an empirical study requiring reliable data; U. S. data are well developed and easily accessible. Third, the United States is reasonably homogeneous and has a large enough and sufficiently "closed" economy so that the influence of the rest of the world is actually quite small.

The justification for not going much beyond fifty years has to do with the belief that radically new technologies can and will arise which will invalidate longer-range projections. For example, the development of nuclear-fusion power would lead to a situation in which energy would be practically inexhaustible; this in turn would alter many other considerations.

Axioms

The basic assumptions underlying the study are similar to those underlying standard economic analysis; that is, that people behave rationally, that they attempt to maximize their utility, that they want more and not less of any good, and that a growth of welfare is desirable. People express their behavior by and large in the marketplace and in the political arena. Their purchases determine what manufacturers will produce, and their voting behavior determines political decisions. Our study is not a normative study. We do not try to suggest that one kind of behavior is better than another. We accept society as it is—a society which is interested in material welfare and a high standard of living.

Our questions began to take the following shape:

What are the welfare consequences of various modes of population growth and economic growth, and what are the welfare consequences of the various methods that can be employed in order to influence economic growth?

It should be recognized that economic growth can be influenced by a variety of methods. If, for example, we wish to stop economic growth, the method employed is important because the welfare consequences are determined by it. Consider, for example, the following ways in which growth of Gross National Product can be affected:

1. By influencing population growth.

2. By changing the savings rate, and thereby the rate of investment.

3. By stimulating or discouraging technical innovation and technological progress.

4. By rationing or taxing energy consumption.

5. By introducing more leisure by means of enforcing early retirement, or by encouraging late entry into the work force.

6. One might even postulate a situation in which work is outlawed for men, thus making up for centuries of discrimination against females.

7. Finally, government can influence economic growth through its fiscal and monetary policies.

Objectives of the study

The objectives of the study are twofold: (1) to construct an objective function—a "target"—which measures the total amount of "welfare" per individual in the nation. The definition of "welfare" must be appropriate to our society and cultural patterns. It must also be a reasonably operational definition so that welfare can be approximated from the kind of data that are available in the national statistics. (2) To develop a mathematical model which relates the index of welfare to demographic and economic parameters, thus allowing us to project a time "stream" of welfare indices as a function of various assumptions concerning population levels and the structure and level of the economy.

Construction of a welfare index

One might object that the index of welfare which we are defining does not really measure happiness. It roughly measures, however, an important component of happiness: the "global" or impersonal component. The other component is intensely local and is determined by interpersonal interactions with a very few people, with family, co-workers, friends, etc. The personal component in the quality of life may be reasonably independent of overall demographic and economic parameters. If this is so, we need not try to include it in our partial analysis.

The construction of a welfare index follows in concept the ideas of Juster (NBER), Nordhaus and Tobin (Yale), and others who would "amputate and impute the GNP." However, we depart considerably from previous work. Like most others, we define welfare as consumption in households. We include nonmarket or household goods (except for illegal services and goods which are not counted by the official national income statisticians either). We add in the value of leisure—not at the opportunity cost of wages forgone, but using an empirical utility function, based on what people indicate their leisure time is worth. Although we count much of educational expense as investment and not as consumption, we ascribe health costs to consumption rather than to investment or to "regrettable necessities." Such items as defense expenditures, police expenditures, and commuting to work are all regrettable necessities and are not counted in our welfare total. Every item that enters into GNP, i.e., every item of governmental and private expenditures, is classified in this manner.

Certain disamenities which are produced by population and economic growth are treated as subtractions from welfare. (1) For example, there are pollution-control costs which tend to rise faster than the GNP. In spite of the fact that there is a trend away from goods production and toward services, and in spite of the fact that processes are being introduced that create less pollution, the limited assimilative capacity of the air and water environment introduces an important nonlinearity which cannot be escaped. (2) Resource costs also increase as items such as fossil fuels become exhausted. In a perfect market, there would of course be immediate substitutions or the immediate introduction of new technology. In the existing imperfect markets there is a kind of "stickiness" (akin to static friction) which slowly "ratches up" the cost. We are now seeing this phenomenon appear in the trend of oil and gas prices. (3) Finally, we have the congestion costs associated with population growth. Large cities become increasingly less efficient as traffic jams increase internal distribution costs; as land prices and rents rise; and as interpersonal disamenities, such as crime and all kinds of urban problems, increase. Of course, some of these disutilities could be ameliorated by technology; for example, by a better transportation system. But we have to take account of the increasing inefficiencies which raise the cost of living and diminish per capita welfare as population and GNP grow.

There is obviously much arbitrariness in the definition of an index of welfare. I have called our measure the Q-index rather than the welfare or quality-of-life index, simply because many people have already formed their own definitions or opinions on what the index might contain. Although definitions are always a matter of taste, I hope that reasonable people may agree that the concept is at least a better measure of welfare than GNP. I hope, however, that I have not been guilty of what St. Augustine confessed:

> For so it is, oh Lord my God, I measure it; but what it
> is that I measure I do not know.

Construction of
the mathematical model

Our mathematical model consists of three parts. The demographic part is rather complicated, yet conceptually quite straightforward. It considers native and immigrant populations and their age distributions. It incorporates different assumptions concerning fertility rates. The model projects its characteristics of households, the geographic distribution of population, the income distribution, and the labor productivities in different sectors (agriculture, manufacturing, services and government). By considering labor-participation rates and trends, it projects the effective labor supply.

The economic part of the model is a very aggregative, essentially neoclassical model with one basic output—GNP. Part of the GNP is reinvested in net new capital which leads to rising productivity because it incorporates technological progress. The model allows for different behavior of the investment function, including one which preserves a constant capital-labor ratio.

The third part of the model is a diagnostic tool that calculates the welfare index. The output of the economy is divided according to demand sectors, i.e., households, investment, etc. Each sector is then analyzed along the definition of our welfare index. The output is also divided by the sectors responsible for the production so as to calculate the resource and environmental implications and the resource and environmental costs.

I will not draw any comparisons here between our model and that of the Club of Rome group at MIT. Suffice it to say that our model does not attempt a worldwide aggregation, nor do we aggregate all resources, all pollution, etc. Instead we have done our aggregation at the economic level, using dollar values as the common unit. This essentially is the philosophy underlying the measure of GNP which aggregates goods and services of various kinds. Our model attempts to simulate the operation of our market economy as closely as possible.

Results

There are many kinds of results. Suppose we visualize a typical printout from a computer run. The assumptions are shown in the legend; nevertheless, we shall comment on some of the more prominent results. The main result of our run is that per capita welfare is increasing today and that it will continue to increase for some time to come before it reaches a maximum. However, much can happen in the way of technological change which makes projections beyond thirty to fifty years quite uncertain. Of particular interest are the different results obtained by running the model with one of the main assumptions slightly changed. Since we are primarily interested in the effects of population growth, let us present the results from two runs based on different fertility assumptions. Run A assumes that the 1968 fertility rate remains unchanged. Run B assumes that the fertility rate diminishes to two-thirds of this value asymptotically, with a half-time of ten years. A comparison of Run A with Run B shows that the slower rate of population growth leads to higher benefits at all times in the future.

General comments on results

What the model does for us is to provide a diagnostic tool which allows us to total up the welfare effects of any particular assumption, or governmental policy, or private decision, etc. It sums the pluses and the minuses and compares them eventually in the Q-index, which is the important objective function. The result is a time run of Q-indices. The larger values are clearly more desirable; the smaller ones are less desirable. Interesting situations arise when Q-indices based on different policies intersect over time. There are many practical examples for such situations. A large capital investment over the next few years would reduce present consumption and therefore temporarily lower the Q-index. Presumably, however, the Q-index in future years would be higher than if the capital investment had not been undertaken.

Our model provides an explicit method of looking at the future and evaluating the consequences of a policy decision. In our example, one would compare two streams of welfare benefits which have been calculated by the computer model. To make such a comparison, however, future benefits must be discounted. Our model cannot determine the discount rate. It is set by considerations which are largely socio-economic, and it is partly determined by how much we feel we owe to future generations. Some have argued that since future generations will be wealthier and better off than we are and will certainly have a higher welfare index, then taxing ourselves now to benefit a future generation amounts to regressive taxation. As the old saying goes, "What has posterity ever done for us?"

There are, of course, many examples in which discounted future benefits compared to present costs need to be considered. In pollution control, for example, the separation of sanitary and storm sewers in U. S. cities may cost between 30 and 50 billion dollars. The restoration of the Great Lakes may be a project of equal magnitude. Should we undertake such a project, and over what time scale?

There are still many weaknesses in our model. We are aware of some of these. We have not yet taken into account the distribution of income and the distribution of welfare; at present the model deals only with averages. We have no theory of how growth affects distribution of income, nor do we have a theory of how distribution of income affects growth (perhaps by way of productivity or through the absence of strikes and social upheavals). Knowledge of the distribution of income is important because it affects consumption patterns. Higher income means more luxury goods and more services, relative to basic necessities.

We have not quite discovered how to compare one distribution of welfare with another; neither have we been able to take into account the "Dusenberry effect" of the disutility involved in the invidious comparison of unequal incomes. Until then we must use the concept of cardinal welfare value. We plan to do some experimentation on discretionary welfare, defined as welfare beyond the basic necessities of life.

At this stage the input-output table has not yet been introduced. We are therefore not yet in a position to have consistent interindustry forecasts of the kind carried out by Clopper Almon. It is our hope that we may be able to introduce this feature very soon.

Summary

We have taken some steps to construct a diagnostic tool to measure the social consequences of decision-making, technology assessment, and population policies. By focusing on a single Q-index which roughly measures welfare, we hope to be able to answer the question whether we as a society will be better off or worse off, given varying sets of assumptions, under one set of policies or another set of policies, with one technology as against another technology, and with one set of private decisions, e.g., regarding fertility, as against another set. In particular, we hope to be able to give some guides as to which combinations of demographic parameters lead to a maximum value of the welfare index.

9 | Discussion of the papers

THIS SECTION presents the formal reactions of selected discussants to certain of the papers already presented in this volume. Each discussant was chosen for his expertise in the field of inquiry covered by the respective papers. Jay Anderson and Joel Darmstadter discuss the papers by Kranzberg and Gerber. David Amidon and Simon Rottenberg comment on the contributions of Goldman and Day. Barry Chiswick and Richard Easterlin discuss the papers presented by Thurow and Singer.

JAY ANDERSON

It is an honor and a privilege to participate in this symposium. You must, of course, realize that I am here as a chemist, not as an economist, nor as an historian, and only as a rank amateur theologian. When I tried to compose my thoughts on Professor Kranzberg's paper, I thought that a suitable title for my response might be "Industrial Humanism: Salvation by the Skin of Our Teeth." I was thinking in particular of Thornton Wilder's play *The Skin of Our Teeth*, which has just that kind of salvation built into it. It is a hopeful play; certainly Kranzberg is very hopeful. I am hopeful too, but that is because I am an amateur theologian, although I am also a professional pessimist.

I would like to emphasize a point which is not one of disagreement between myself and Kranzberg: the role of social institutions. He is certainly correct in asserting that the world model which appears in *The Limits to Growth* is unhistorical or ahistorical in that it neglects social variables. There are no parameters that we can follow to monitor the development of social institutions. Social simulation as a technique is still in its infancy, and *The Limits to Growth* study made no attempt to bring that kind of work into its model. It is almost exclusively a physical model, which prompts me to remark that the kind of growth which we want to limit is strictly physical growth: throughput of material goods from resources to waste or pollution, and the throughput of human beings from cradle to grave. It should be understood, however, that the model provides for and indeed assumes continued growth in many non-physical areas.

The basic question that we need to wrestle with is that which Kranzberg raised: Can man's technological creativity continue indefinitely to enable him to overcome the obstacles to physical growth? Professor Mishan has his doubts; I would like to share one of the primary reasons why I have my doubts as well. They arise because of what we refer to in system dynamics vocabulary as *physical and social delays*. Let me give you some examples of delays. The study on the translocation of mercury through the environment, which my wife and I did at MIT,[1] identifies a number of physical delays. It takes about a year for mercury levels that build up in the atmosphere to be washed out. It takes several decades for mercury levels that build up in the fresh water system to be washed out. It will take several centuries before mercury levels which may build up in the oceans can be removed. These are examples of physical delays, and I submit that they are delays which are not susceptible to technological change; they are part of the physical environment, and probably are something which cannot be meddled with through our technology.

There are also social delays. The following is a trivial example, but it helps illustrate the point. This year, in the pole-vault competition at the Olympic Games in Munich, Bob Seagram was about to clear eighteen feet with a fiber-glass pole. The fiber-glass pole, in a sense, represents a technological breakthrough which would have allowed a limit to growth—eighteen feet in the pole vault—to be broken. However, for purely political reasons (so the television commentators told us), he was not permitted to use the fiber-glass pole. Thus, until that political or social process has been worked out, that limit to growth will not be broken. One of the things which I think the historical perspective does not allow us to get a grasp on is the relationship between these very real delays in the operation of the social or physical system and the rise of population, capital, etc. If, for example, it is true that our demand for energy is doubling every six or seven years, and if it takes more than six or seven years to get communities to agree on nuclear-power-plant siting and other factors necessary to implement the new facilities, then indeed the limit to growth will be reached: there will be brownouts or blackouts. These do not occur because of the failure of technology, but because of the delay that operates within the social system.

It is for this reason, and almost for this reason alone, that the world model comes up with its very sorrowful predictions of what we call "overshoot and collapse." It is because of the operation of delays in the face of growth that the world system does not reach a happy equilibrium smoothly, but rather overshoots the carrying capacity of the globe and then declines below that capacity.

167

Incidentally, I wonder whether or not there are models that allow for a smooth rise of population and capital accumulation to a natural physical limit. I recently read a description of just such a model in a paper by Ayres and Kneese.[2] In order to accommodate a smooth rise of population to a natural limit of about 15-20 billion people by the middle of the twenty-first century, and a smooth rise of capital to a per capita income comparable to that which we Americans enjoy today by that same time, it was necessary to implement not only a great number of technological achievements which we are just beginning to hear about, but also a number of social controls. Here is the point on which I can have no debate with Professor Kranzberg. Technology in the absence of shifts in the social system is not an adequate technique for assuring either growth or a better life. Some of the social controls that he spoke of, and that of technology assessment in particular, are precisely what *The Limits to Growth* is talking about. In fact, a technology assessment could be a kind of control that would limit growth. If, on assessing a technology, we decide that we don't want it (consider the SST, for example), then that will represent a way of limiting growth. Popular control of technology, the notion of a participatory democracy that would be able to control the devices of its scientific establishment, is a mechanism by which growth will be limited.

The Limits to Growth is not anti-technology; it does not advocate a moratorium on technological progress. Rather, it suggests that at present technology, in the face of rising growth, serves only to defer the limits to growth; it serves only to defer problems further into the future, without becoming ultimately responsible for them. The study is critical of the price system as a tool for evaluating the scarcity of resources or evaluating the effects of pollution or other externalities because there is no way, as far as I know, to evaluate the future, to make the future commensurable with the present. The future is an externality, but one which ought to be internalized. This is very difficult to do, and it has not been done.

Technology in a steady-state system, rather than in a growing system, is not used simply to defer limits to growth, but rather to choose between alternatives: to choose between different combinations of life styles, between different levels of capital, population or food production, between different ways to use our capital stocks that could be consistent with the popular will. *The Limits to Growth* is not against technology; it says that technology should be used to open alternatives whereas, in the face of continuing growth, technology is used instead to defer limits to growth. Technology must meet needs in the face of an impending crisis, and hence there is neither time nor room to search for alternatives.

Finally, I would like to call your attention to an issue which has only barely begun to emerge in the symposium: the elitist aspect of our deliberations. Who is it who will decide upon values? Does growth or a steady-state world impose more or fewer restrictions? Who will decide which path is more desirable? I am told that one way of measuring energy consumption is the comparison that in ancient Greece the noble families used about ten slaves per person, while now in America we use the energy equivalent of about two hundred slaves per person. Where are those slaves coming from? Are they coming from the Middle East, which supplies us our oil? Are they coming from the Navaho tribes of Utah and Arizona, whose land is being strip-mined to supply coal to fuel power plants? Whom are we enslaving at the price of our growth? Whom might we enslave if we stop? Who are we to say that a national park or a pure river is a better thing than a higher standard of living for the developing world? Perhaps the debate on continued economic growth should speak to these questions as well.

Notes

[1] A. A. Anderson, J. M. Anderson, and L. E. Mayer, "System Simulation to Identify Environmental Research Needs: Mercury Contamination, *Oikos 24* (1973); also appearing in D. L. Meadows and D. H. Meadows (eds.), *Toward Global Equilibrium: Collected Papers* (Cambridge, Mass.: Wright-Allen Press, 1973).

[2] R. U. Ayres and A. V. Kneese, "Economic and Ecological Effects of a Stationary Economy," *1971 Annual Review of Ecology and Systematics 2*, 1; also available as reprint 99 from Resources for the Future.

JOEL DARMSTADTER

Professor Kranzberg correctly and pointedly reminds us of numerous historical instances—for example, in the fields of agriculture and mineral resources—in which science and technology succeeded in rescuing society from hardships which some had seemed to sense were preordained. Kranzberg could have gone a step further to note how reliance on technology constitutes a very important element in the stable-state society urged upon us in *The Limits to Growth*. For even a stable economy demands a flow of throughput to sustain some minimal level of personal consumption and wearing down of capital. And how to insure that this inescapable flow of production and consumption accords with both minimal damage to the natural environment and the least drawdown of our stock of nonrenewable resources? Why, through technological progress of course—first, to minimize the volume of this throughput by designing products that last longer or are susceptible to recycling; second, to permit the eventual, but inexorable, recourse to extraction of less-accessible ore bodies; and third, to guard ourselves against the situation in which even a zero rate of growth in GNP holds no assurance that a cumulative despoliation of the environment will not upset the balance between economic activity and the ecological system which we seek to preserve. It is hard to see, incidentally, how this threefold set of conditions could be met without growing use of energy.

In other words, what *The Limits to Growth* position signifies is the same plea for "buying time" that other, less apocalyptic, persons insist is necessary to devise solutions for problems that will greet us in the next round of man's existence—"getting a technological fix on things," to use one of the more disagreeable bits of contemporary jargon. Except, of course, that the Meadows group is persuaded that drastic and monumental change is necessary within an exceedingly short span of time, whereas others are more sanguine about the breathing space allotted to us to work things out.

Having so far concurred with the main thrust of Kranzberg's remarks and been receptive to his evocation of historical analogy, I am nevertheless uneasy about just where recourse to historical precedent begins to lose its reliability. Specifically, what methodological mechanism exists that alerts the analyst to phenomena that may perhaps be incapable of being dealt with simply by historical examples? The management of civilian nuclear energy, for example, seems to me to be a case so markedly unique as to defy comparison with any analogous challenges of the past. Growing stockpiles of radioactive materials will be subject to release or misuse. The problem of nuclear-waste management is difficult enough for the United States, with its command over a complex technology and its endowment of a stable social and political order, let alone for the dozens of nations in the world that are likely soon to acquire nuclear power reactors within their borders.

According to the International Atomic Energy Agency, over one-half of worldwide electric power output may be atomic by the year 2000. According to U. S. government estimates, by 1990 the United States will have to locate sites for about 165 new nuclear plants, all of them over 500 mw capacity, with a significant portion exceeding 3,000 mw. If the projection of worldwide nuclear generating capacity by the end of the century at 3.2 million mw is reasonable, it is equally reasonable to expect the presence by that time of some 3,200 large nuclear power stations (assuming average capacity of 1,000 mw) around the globe. Where nuclear-fuel management occurs in countries with political instability or less sophisticated technological traditions, the normal problems of nuclear-fuel handling may therefore be compounded. The assumption behind the quantitative estimates is that breeder reactors will take on an increasingly important role; thus, the monitoring and containment of plutonium—potentially a source of nuclear weaponry—will become an enormous responsibility.

I cite this example because the nuclear-based energy future which is often portrayed for us with such salesmanlike enthusiasm frequently neglects this unprecedented aspect of the problem, perhaps because there is really no powerful historical antecedent with which to allay our fears.

I agree with Mr. Gerber that, if we sidestep debating the desirability of growth versus no-growth, a growing economy demands a growing utilization of energy resources, both to sustain the rise in productivity and to satisfy the growing level of consumption that increased income permits. Certainly, the question of growth versus no-growth should be evaluated on its broad merits and not be reduced to its implications simply for energy. Conversely, one can conceive of opportunities for the conservation of energy resources that are not primarily the result of a purposeful policy to save on energy. Thus the diversion, over a reasonable period of time, of a substantial portion of intraurban automotive transport to some form of mass transit would, I think, be beneficial to many aspects of urban living, quite aside from the very considerable net savings in energy which may thereby accrue.

That such potential energy savings exist, and that they may be realized without infringing on the welfare and hopes of either poor people or of society as a whole, should, however, be recognized; it is in this respect that Mr. Gerber's paper might have been somewhat more assertive. Mercifully, he did not go so far as some trade journals or utility executives who would have us think that, were it not for that last Btu of energy, this country would forfeit its preeminence in all things that matter—a status which, it is claimed, is attributable to the abundant and cheap fuel and power conferred upon us throughout history.

Perhaps the energy-conservation possibilities that we can consider are at present rather modest, when judged by annual volumes of consumption and year-to-year increments. Yet at a time when we are severely pressed to add to our domestic oil and gas reserves, to overcome technological obstacles to the environmentally acceptable use of coal, to overcome problems besetting the production of nuclear power and the siting and thermal-discharge problems associated with all electric generation, I believe a sober look at conservation is not at all amiss. Particularly if—and I revert to my earlier remarks—it helps us buy time for perfecting solutions to resource insufficiency through such things as coal gasification, breeders, and—more distant—solar and fusion power.

What are some examples of energy-saving opportunities? No less an authority than the Association of Heating, Refrigeration, and Air-Conditioning Engineers—scarcely what you would call a bunch of environmental freaks—can be cited to document the substantial variations in efficiency (i.e., the relationship between the Btu's of cooling put out and the wattage absorbed) of air-conditioning units—variations not explainable by cost differences. The American public has virtually no familiarity with this efficiency aspect of air conditioning. Why not a mandatory labeling requirement certifying the efficiency and, perhaps also, the cost of running air conditioners? This would inform the potential customer of the amount of unnecessary energy he consumes and pays for. There is no reason why manufacturers would not quickly respond to this new factor in merchandising once it is forced on them.

Illumination is another area to consider. It is alleged by architects, whom I have a disposition to respect, that much waste is engendered by the illumination standards which lighting engineering societies succeed in imposing on builders—standards way out of proportion to the physiological requirements of building employees or residents. Moreover, excess lighting generates excess heat that requires additional air conditioning to dissipate.

There is evidence that improved thermal-insulation standards in new buildings could, in a surprisingly short pay-back period, recapture in fuel-cost savings the higher initial outlay for better insulation.

And then, of course, we have the example of the inordinate amount of energy consumed by large-horsepower automobiles, driven daily by their sole occupants in bumper-to-bumper, stop-and-go urban traffic. The efficiency advantages—hence, energy savings—in alternative modes of transport have been graphically demonstrated. Even allowing for the enormous extent to which our city design, housing, and daily lives continue to be conditioned by the automobile, it seems to me inconceivable that a significant shift toward less energy-intensive transport could not be achieved once the recognition of the social cost of unrestricted use of the private passenger car sank into the public consciousness and led us to the adoption of effective disincentives against it.

A hypothetical calculation of the maximum energy savings possible in these and numerous other applications appears in a recent report by the U. S. Office of Emergency Preparedness. In what is clearly very much an outer limit, a figure of over 7 million barrels per day oil equivalent in 1980 is indicated in this study—about 15 percent of aggregate U. S. energy consumption projected for that year. The figure is obviously a hypothetical ideal, for it is arrived at without much attention to the feasibility of the transitional political and social changes necessary for its attainment. Nevertheless, it is incumbent upon us to dissect this analysis carefully to determine which of the proposed conservation opportunities can realistically be attempted. In all these things, change can probably occur only gradually and, in some cases, only as a proportion of incremental demand for energy-associated goods and services. Short of the imposition of standards which would be economically costly and politically coercive, existing homeowners, for example, are not about to bow to exhortation to add calking, weather-stripping and storm windows to their premises. But over time sizable results might be achieved. After all, we have been talking here about energy uses that represent a measurable portion of the nation's annual consumption. At the very least, then, systematic quantitative analysis is called for; neither the proponents nor the debunkers of the conservation argument have as yet revealed much more than intuitive judgments on which to fall back. In that sense, the OEP report is a solid start.

I wish, finally, that Mr. Gerber had provided us with a somewhat less cavalier dismissal of the impact of price change on energy use. There is in this area, as in the conservation argument, some burden of proof falling upon those who would deny any prospect of a significant tie between price rise and dampened demand. I am not speaking necessarily of the matter of restructuring or inverting utility rate schedules, an issue whose many-sided complexity I freely acknowledge. (Though I do believe that the possibilities of peak-use price penalties, common in other countries, need not be lightly shrugged off.) I refer to the more general question of the consequences of prospectively increasing real costs and prices for electricity and other energy forms. Take the matter of electric-power demand. The fact that an analyst forecasting 1970 levels of electricity demand in the mid-1960s would have come exceedingly close to the mark had he done no more than extrapolate the more than 7 percent rate of growth of the preceding five years would seem to lend credence to the proposition that projections based upon historical extrapolations give at least as accurate, if not better, results than those utilizing more complicated assumptions. If, however, presumed historical causal factors are now going to undergo a significant break in trends, then our reliance on what in the past may have been effective electricity forecasting could be seriously misplaced.

Electricity prices have declined steadily in the past several decades while most prices (including those of competing fuels) were generally, if not always, increasing. The presumption now is that the real price of electricity will cease declining and—under the impact of a variety of environmental costs—will henceforth tend to increase, perhaps at a substantial rate.

With such upward price pressures in the cards, it is relevant to ask: What is the short- and long-run price elasticity of demand for electricity? That is, how will demand react to rising prices? A number of analysts are beginning to address themselves to the task of studying this important question. The results to date, disconcertingly varied as to range of estimates, are suggestive rather than conclusive. Nonetheless, it is worth noting that a number of studies point to an unmistakable demand dampening in response to rising prices. The responsiveness of *total* energy demand to changes in energy prices overall is, of course, likely to be less than that for electricity alone, since it is more difficult to substitute for, or do without, energy in general than to do so for one particular type of energy. Also, since people are not easily uncoupled from their electricity-using possessions, an adjustment period is clearly indicated; and, as Mr. Gerber points out, the increased demand induced by rising income works in an opposite direction. Econometric estimates suggest, however, that the income effect is less than offsetting. On balance, it is hard to believe that there would be no overall long-term response whatsoever.

If, in addition to assumptions about price increases, one were to assume a gradual slowdown in GNP and population growth, still further reductions in demand would, of course, be implied. Even without an assured deceleration in GNP growth, there is some evidence that the historical relationship between kilowatt-hours and GNP has not been totally perceived in electric power projections. Applying a statistical regression between the two for the period 1947-1971, a projection of 4 percent GNP growth to the year 2000 yields 5 percent growth in electric power. The Federal Power Commission, however, projects a 6.5 percent growth rate in electric power, and all this does not consider the real possibility of a concerted policy to restrain demand growth.

But rather than engage in arithmetic jousting, what I want to suggest here is that there may be a disinclination to look open-mindedly and searchingly at factors likely to involve breaks with the past. In the case of load forecasting, such myopia (if it truly exists) would simply fortify the arguments of those electric power antagonists who sense a fixation on the sacredness of extrapolated growth rates, irrespective of demonstrable changes in underlying conditions of growth. Moreover, in utility-load forecasting, such a situation (again, if true) could have perniciously self-fulfilling consequences insofar as the capacity, once on line, could impose strong pressure on those obliged to promote its maximum use. It could also force us into exercising prematurely, and perhaps therefore uneconomically, certain options predicated to a large extent on high expected electricity demand.

DAVID AMIDON

My initial reaction to the papers of both Marshall Goldman and Lincoln Day was that they were very interesting reading and presented me with none of the problems of interpreting data that I had anticipated. However, I have the serious problem of not being an economist. Of course, about a decade ago, an inconclusive attempt was made to train me as an historian. Most recently I manifested that training by appearing as a discussant at a meeting of the American Anthropological Association. Somehow I feel that my presence here is an obvious extension of that activity; moreover, if any of you know of any geographers who are planning meetings, please let me know. The obvious problem of a person who comes to a discipline from the outside is that he is necessarily ignorant of the context in which a paper is written, both in the sense that he is not fully apprised of the debate that has been going on within the discipline and also in the sense that he is usually unaware of other work done by the author which might permit him to make more sense of the present paper. I confess to these liabilities. On the other hand, I hope to bring in some fresh perspectives.

In regard to Marshall Goldman's paper, I find his straightforward analysis of growth attitudes in socialist and "Third World" nations persuasive and attractively presented; however, one of my reactions to his paper concerns his choice of problems within the broader context of his area of research. Before pursuing that, let me review some of his extemporaneous remarks. He said that he is addressing himself to radicals. He mentioned Douglas Dowd and Barry Commoner, and says that they ascribe the problems of pollution and growth to capitalism and argue that the problems of pollution can't be solved within the capitalist system. Goldman ought to have added that these men think nothing can be solved in the capitalist system; moreover, if such men were not embracing the "growth crisis," one suspects that they would be looking for some other crisis in order to justify the destruction of capitalism.

Let us turn to another basic question. Goldman shows us that the Soviets have as many problems, or perhaps more problems, than we have. I am especially intrigued by his statement that the Soviets, in some respects, bear responsibility for having started the modern growth mania in the 1920s and for expanding growth consciousness and inspiring rivalry along these lines ever since. I can recall from the summer of 1960, during the Kennedy-Nixon campaign, evenings spent in a graduate student lounge at the University of Pennsylvania in the company of a trio of British graduate students, listening to Kennedy talk about the need to "get this country moving forward again." My foreign friends assured me with relish that capitalism obviously held diminishing hope of forward movement; nevertheless, forward movement was a good thing and under socialism it would happen most quickly. However, I also recall Warren Nutter's writings of the time. He was a prophet against the general Western gloom, crying out that in reality the capitalists knew how to move forward better than the communists and were doing so right along; he suggested that the "forward movement gap," like the "missile gap," was a Kennedy trick. Goldman would agree that the American penchant for economic growth is much older than either Simon Kuznets' GNP concept or the Soviet Five-Year Plans; nevertheless, he is surely right when he says that the Soviet model has been a poor one in the past. Goldman also describes the intransigence of underdeveloped societies when it is suggested to them that they should deliberately forgo the possibilities of growth. All of this tends to support a seemingly clinical and dispassionate "judgment" that deliberate limitation of growth is impossible. Goldman seems to suggest that because the Soviets don't want to stop growing (quite the contrary) and because the economically backward areas want to grow, somehow this undercuts the desirability of trying to stop growth. I think that these are very separate questions. We must discuss the question of norms, the question of what is desirable, somewhat apart from the question of what is possible. We ought to consider the possibility that if the Soviet Union and the underdeveloped nations are going to oppose limiting growth, and if limiting growth is nevertheless deemed desirable, then expertise such as Goldman's should be enlisted in a struggle to overcome such opposition. The intransigence of the Third World and of the Soviet Union joins the list of problems to be solved by those who would stop growth, if growth indeed is to be stopped.

Of course, Goldman has simply chosen not to discuss very much at all the question of whether stopping growth or limiting it is desirable. Rather, he has assumed that it is desirable to stop or limit growth and has gone on to tell us that neither is going to happen. This leaves us still puzzled concerning the question that I hoped his paper would answer, namely: Will a postgrowth world, if one ever comes to pass, also be an anti- or postcapitalist world? The question, it seems to me, is probably to be answered in the affirmative. The price system, which is thought by many to be the heart of capitalism, is everywhere giving way to a kind of managed economy, in which allocations of things are more and more politically determined. This is happening in our own society, where the market model seems to diverge increasingly from reality. Surely this tendency will be accelerated by any deliberate attempt to limit or reverse growth. Such a policy would call for more explicit intervention in economic processes; it would seem inevitably to entail fuller politicization of the process of ordering economic priorities. In short, a low-growth or no-growth world may have little to learn from the Soviet version of "socialism," but it will probably involve further mutations away from the free market model.

Professor Day's paper, which is utopian throughout, winds up with a discussion of how the lambs will lie down with the lions and how there will be less international conflict in the event of reduced economic growth. I would suggest that something almost diametrically opposite is the case, namely, that there will continue to be virtually irresistible worldwide commitment to growth precisely so long as there is chronic and intense international conflict. In other words, a critical obstacle in the way of anti-growth policies in the most advanced nation-states is the attachment of rival blocs to theories about the relatedness of economics and power and prestige, which they hold with as much zeal as the crusaders of old; what we have here is a modern holy war in the sphere of the provision of economic goods. In the presence of this holy war, and until we can reduce its quasi-religious dimension, every opportunity which seems to afford a chance to increase power is seized upon by the contenders, whether reluctantly or cheerfully, on the grounds that anything that might enable a nation to enhance its power simply cannot be neglected as a possible advantage in the ongoing conflict. Growth, of course, is generally supposed to contribute fairly directly to increased national power. I would say, then, that it is idle to suppose that a commitment to control growth can be achieved prior to and as a means of bringing about a reduction in international tensions; it would rather seem to me that a reduction of severe international tensions must have the priority in the solution of the problem.

I would say about Mr. Day's paper that, in general, it sounds like a description of an ideal world (to which the liberal side of me is attracted), into which has been plugged the phenomenon of reduced growth as a general cause for bringing about everything that contemporary academic liberals ever hoped for. Day's utopian vision tends to reflect the values of that growing middle class group which exists by providing expanding services in such realms as education and social welfare work, and which is generally anti-market and anti-business in its attitudes. I can't suppress the feeling that Day has happened upon the necessity for suppressing growth as a happy answer to the question: "How are we going to get rid of all those bad guys who make their livings by buying and selling?" One is reminded of the ideal commonwealth created by Edward Bellamy in 1889, in his book *Looking Backward;* Bellamy, an unsuccessful law student, imagined a utopian future in which there were no lawyers (or bankers or barkeepers). In Day's vision of the post-growth world, there are few salesmen and stockbrokers and apparently no advertising men. What academician will not, in his heart, say good riddance to these classic enemies of our group? "Enemies," of course, because they seem to have made fundamentally different choices as to values and life styles.

This light treatment of Mr. Day's work is not meant to convey lack of respect for his very real achievement. Day has been remarkably resourceful in imagining the manifold implications of adopting a ZEG policy. "Futurism" is lately spoken of as a legitimate field of academic inquiry, and Lincoln Day obviously possesses great talents along these lines. Indeed, I am personally much attracted to his position. Yet it was wariness of the spell cast by Day which led me to heightened awareness of the possible extent to which reactions to the growth controversy may be a function of basic, pre-existing value commitments.

Marshall Goldman implied in his paper, and stated explicitly in his extemporaneous remarks, that the growth question will not be solved by academic debaters in pleasant circumstances (who aren't even wondering whether dinner will be there tonight); rather, the problem will ultimately be solved (if that is the right word) by the event itself, that is, the actual collapse of one or more dimensions of the present world system, in which case some solutions will have to be found—given any survivors. The probability is that no "solutions" will be taken seriously until and unless history vindicates the anti-growth prophets of doom; thus, practically speaking, there are no answers to the question raised here. It might seem surprising that so many serious men have felt constrained to take strong positions on issues which are moot so far as any prospect for real change in national policy is concerned. I believe that inquiry into the question of scholarly motivation in this irresoluble controversy offers one of the most fruitful lines of investigation connected with the great growth debate.

Why do the "growths" *want* so badly to believe that growth can continue indefinitely, that yet-undeveloped technologies will brush aside developing crises? On the other hand, why do the "zeros" *want* so badly to believe that the absence of growth, or even its reversal, is both necessary and desirable? I will offer an explanation that comes out of my own background as a person who has been reading intensively in the area of ethnic studies and ethno-cultural groups in the United States. Put in bold and half-facetious terms, I would suggest that what we have here is a conflict between Christian engineers and Jewish economists. The former are symbolized by Jay Forrester and the Club of Rome group; the latter are represented by Professor Solow, among many others. Obviously this dichotomy is very crude, with many exceptions, but I do believe that cultural ("tribal") groups have values which perpetuate themselves many generations past the period at which individuals in the group are comfortably identified with religious propositions. Thus, one may be a third-generation agnostic of Protestant ancestry and still be profoundly influenced by cultural strands that are intrinsic to one of the various Protestant traditions. It seems to me that what we have here is, in part, a tradition of respect for asceticism (in principle, if decidedly not in practice), possibly extending in the case of some anti-growth people to include an unconscious belief in the virtue of suffering. Such views surface even among Christian Socialists. The Christian Socialist might maintain that the redistribution of wealth was a good idea, but I think that very often he was really, instinctively, talking about the redistribution of poverty. Jewish Socialists, on the other hand, have had on the whole a more positive orientation toward the things of this world and are relatively unconcerned about the hereafter, the rejection of the material world, the mortification of the flesh, and so on. They have had no trouble in seeing the distribution of *wealth* as the real problem of social change. I think there is a tendency on the part of the anti-growth people to welcome a little too warmly the image of a future in which the evil material goods of this world will somehow be swept away and an idyllic pastoral scene will be restored. On the other hand, no doubt, there is a tendency on the part of pro-growth people to be too uncritical of the times in which we live, in which things *are* in the saddle and riding hard.

One parting word as far as future policy is concerned: I don't think we need to look so much to the Third World or the Soviet Union in the area of future policy. I think we have to look at ourselves and think about instituting some changes in this country, because we are the Joneses with whom the rest of the world is trying to keep up. We must make our own effort to seriously discipline some of the most anti-environmental aspects of our culture. Admittedly this will not solve the world problems if India and China continue to dump thousands of tons of DDT into the oceans; however, it may provide a different kind of model for them to emulate. We are at the center of the world's communication network. Images generated in this country of what the good life is all about are influential around the world. We ought to be generating a different image.

SIMON ROTTENBERG

There seem to be two basic worries running through the discussion at these meetings. One is that the rapid rate of economic growth is exhausting the world's fixed stock of nonrenewable resources too rapidly. The other is that over time the increased output of goods is accompanied by the production of bads. Utilities and disutilities are being jointly produced. The processes that produce things which give pleasure in consumption also produce wastes which are visible and abstrusive and are not easily disposable.

I would like to refer to aspects of both of these worrisome phenomena.

With respect to the exhaustion of nonrenewable resources, there are two possibilities. One is that there is *not* a fixed stock of resources in the world and the other is that there *is* a fixed stock. If there were not a fixed stock—as if we learned how to extract myriad resources from air, or in principle at zero cost, and air were available in infinite quantity—there would be nothing to worry about. It would then be possible for the quantity of resources per capita to rise continuously.

If the command of technical knowledge does not move in that direction or does not move fast enough, then resources *do* come to be nonrenewable and the stock of them becomes fixed. This would be true even if resources are never lost, even if we learned to organize the collection and retransformation of waste through low-cost recycling processes. Under such conditions, the quantity of resources might remain unchanged and it would be composed of a basket of, say, ore still untapped, ore in the process of transformation to steel, steel tubing, bicycles, and used-up bicycles waiting on scrap heaps for recycling into some other fabricated form. Whether the quantity of resources per capita would remain unchanged, or rise or fall, would then depend upon whether the world's population remained unchanged, fell or rose.

If the population of the world rises, or if it remains unchanged and it is found too costly to collect and transform waste, resources per capita will decline. The question then becomes one of determining the appropriate time-rate of consumption from fixed-resource stocks. We might remove resources from the stock at the rate of an ounce per unit of time or at the rate of a ton per unit of time. But whatever the rate of removal, in the end the stock becomes exhausted.

The appropriate rate of consumption of resources is a function of the intensity of the preference for the present over the future or, as it is sometimes expressed, a function of the discount rate. Mr. Goldman says that no observable discount rate takes into account the effects on people who will live twelve generations hence. That is true. But I do not know what moral principle defines the fair sacrifices that people living in the present ought to make on behalf of people who will live in the future. If I am told that people living now do not take into account the interests of those who will live in the distant future, I do not know that this is necessarily unfair. If the interests of the latter *are* taken into account, it means that those living now must make greater sacrifices on behalf of the future than they now do. I do not know what a fair rate of intergenerational transfer of wealth is, and I am not really in a position to say that the discount rates which govern decisions that are observed in the world are unjust or unfair. This is especially true once we note that people living now are much better off in a material sense than their ancestors were and, by extrapolation, that people living in the future will be better off, in the same sense, than people living now. In that context, additional increments of sacrifice by those currently living in order to provide more for those who will live in the future will produce a transfer of wealth from the poor to the rich, and it is not clear to me that such a regressive arrangement will serve the purposes of justice.

It should be noted that the future *does* get taken into account in decisions made in the present consumption. People now frequently make decisions to postpone. Goods are stored for consumption in the future; capital is formed for the production of goods that will appear in the future; saving occurs. A wide variety of postponement decisions are made. These decisions occur in markets and they are guided by price relatives and expected price relatives. It is not true, therefore, that the future is given zero weight in markets as we currently know them. The future does get taken into account, and even though those who will live in the future do not vote directly, they *do* vote through the instrument of people currently voting in markets who decide whether to postpone. The question is whether the quantity of postponement that occurs in markets is sufficient to be "fair," and I know no moral principle that instructs us that the actual rate of postponement is not fair.

The second theme that has run through these meetings is that bads are produced jointly with the production of goods. This is the problem of environmental pollution. There seems to be consensus here that if only external costs were internalized, decisions would tend to be more optimal than they are now and, if they were more optimal, a smaller quantity of pollution would occur.

Some years ago Professor Ronald Coase wrote what has come to be a classic paper, "The Problem of Social Cost," in which he develops the thesis that conditions can be defined in exchange relationships such that the quantity of damaging polluting that is done is the same no matter how the costs of pollution are distributed. Where the cost incides is a function of the liability rule. If the rule causes the cost to fall upon John Doe, he has an incentive to produce some given quantity of damage from pollution and no more than that; if the rule causes the cost to fall upon Richard Roe, *he* has an incentive to produce some quantity of damage from pollution, and the optimal quantity of damage from pollution is the same in both cases.

If there is pollution and it does no damage in any sense, there is no cause for worry. If there is pollution that is damaging, the costs fall upon someone. In that sense they are always internalized. Those upon whom the costs fall have an incentive to avoid costs. Abstracting from questions of equity, and looking only at resource allocational and output effects, the community may be indifferent as between liability rules that cause more abatement of pollution and liability rules that cause "victims" of pollution to remove to other premises where the pollution will do them less damage. Whether the one is to be preferred to the other depends upon the relative costs of the two strategies, and it may frequently be found that diminished damage by removal is preferable to diminished damage by abatement.

I move now to Mr. Day's paper. He says that zero economic growth will produce an idyllic world. I am not convinced that the sort of world he has described would be idyllic; it seems to me that such a world would be a dull and uninteresting one. But beyond that, if he *has* described an idyllic world, it is not clear to me that zero economic growth will cause such a world to come to pass.

Mr. Day says that zero economic growth would cause advertising to be of little significance; the number of salesmen to decline; packaging and commercial design to decline; the number employed in maintenance and repair work to increase; the number of agricultural workers and the variety of personal social services to increase; population to be less highly urbanized; the urban population to be less concentrated in metropolitan areas; less division of labor; less emphasis on "getting ahead"; less desire for second jobs and less acceptance of overtime work; a more positive attitude toward work and more pride in work; more durability and higher quality in products, and less attention to style and obsolescence; and so on and so forth. Now, it is not obvious to me that these things would come about as a result of the achievement of zero-growth rates, and I can conceptualize a world of zero-growth rates in which conditions can be defined that would cause none of these things to happen at all.

There are other peculiar and bizarre things that I find in Mr. Day's paper. In his zero-growth world, he says, we could expect a greater sharing of equipment— from lawn mowers and washing machines to farm machinery and public transportation—and this sharing would generate psychically rewarding experience. If the neighbor does not return the lawn mower on time or breaks it, the sharing may generate psychic disutility, and Mr. Day takes no account of this possible consequence. But quite apart from that, the magnitude of sharing that goes on in our positive-growth-rate world is enormous. The rental market is extraordinarily large in our world, and this means that much sharing of equipment goes on now. Self-employment is a large fraction of all employment; all the clients of an attorney share his investment in the acquisition of legal knowledge and skill. How does Mr. Day know that the quantity of sharing in a zero-growth-rate world will exceed the quantity of sharing observed in positive-growth-rate worlds?

There is nowhere in his paper a formulation of a theory for explaining how durable capital—both tangible and human—is kept busy. Similarly, if people are brought physically closer together by the sharing of public transport facilities, does Mr. Day really know that they will learn from this experience to love, rather than to fear and hate, one another?

There is still more naïveté in his paper. The automobile, he says, insulates man from his environment and from personal contact with others and causes him to be competitive, aggressive, and destructive. If one tends to be dyspeptic, he might see automobiles producing aggressive behavior; those with compassionate and generous natures would, alternatively, see the automobile as an instrument for producing massive cooperation. Indeed, if automobile drivers were not essentially cooperative, would it be possible for expressways and beltways in the United States to carry the enormous flows of traffic that we observe daily? Cannot these traffic flows be taken as evidence of the propensity of drivers to be cooperative and courteous and to take account of the adverse consequences that imprudent driving would impose upon them and upon others?

I am led to conclude that what we have been observing at these meetings is not simply the application of critical intelligence to real and hypothetical states of the world. We have also experienced here the baring of psyches by participants in the symposium. Some are optimistic and compassionate; others are pessimistic and paranoid. The nature of the speaker seems greatly to have affected the quality of verbal utterance that pretends to derive exclusively from the exercise of rational intelligence.

BARRY R. CHISWICK

The link between economic growth and the distribution of income is an old issue. There are two aspects to the causal link. First, what is the effect of the distribution of income on economic growth? Second, what is the effect of economic growth on the distribution of income? I have been asked to comment on the second issue, starting from Lester Thurow's paper "Zero Economic Growth and the Distribution of Income."[1]

Any study of the effect on income distribution of a policy of a specific rate of economic growth, whether zero or positive, must deal with three issues. First, it must define growth and the desired level of growth. Second, it must present one or more means by which the desired objective can be obtained. And third, it must present the income-distribution implications of each scenario. Each step in the analysis is contingent on satisfying the previous step.

A study of the income implications of zero economic growth (ZEG) should indicate the policies by which the government would achieve the target level of growth. Alternative paths to the target level must be specified before we can conclude that zero economic growth implies an increasing inequality of income. Secondly, the statistical analysis should be appropriate and there should be no confusion of cyclical and secular changes in employment.

Thurow defines zero economic growth as no growth in deflated GNP. It is my impression, however, that the advocates of ZEG don't really mean no change in GNP. ZEG advocates (and nonadvocates!) are concerned with the environment and natural resources. They are concerned with the increasing filth of our air, water, streets and countryside, as well as with the depletion of exhaustible natural resources.

A skeptic would ask: To what extent should the present generation sacrifice its consumption so that a future generation can consume more than would otherwise be possible? What are the costs to future generations of current net environmental destruction and how do we translate these future costs into present values? An optimal environmental policy requires an answer to these questions.

Let me present two polar policies: The first is "Damn the future, full speed ahead." The second is that we should bequeath to future generations a world no more dirty (and perhaps a little cleaner!) and resources no more expensive than the world we inherited.[2] Zero net environmental destruction (ZNED) may imply a positive, zero or even negative rate of growth of deflated GNP. Or, put differently, ZEG may imply positive or negative net environmental destruction (NED).

Furthermore, the path taken to zero economic growth may affect the rate of net environmental destruction. Suppose we were to tax activities which destroy the environment, subsidize activities which cleanse the environment, and subsidize research which promotes zero net environmental destruction. The result might well be that we can have ZNED and positive economic growth. For example, with respect to the automobile, a ZEG policy would imply increasing taxes on gasoline (especially gasoline containing lead), increasing the enforcement of antipollution standards on cars, and increasing taxes on minerals extracted from the earth.[3] The taxes would encourage the use of transportation facilities that use less gasoline, that use more recycled materials, and that expel fewer pollutants. An alternative path to ZEG, one with different environmental implications, would be to use monetary and fiscal policies to reduce the rate of growth of GNP. Fewer people would buy new cars. As the average age of cars increases, they consume more gasoline and oil per mile and expel more pollutants per mile. This path to zero economic growth may result in an increase in environmental destruction. Note that these two policies may have different implications for the distribution of income.

These comments are not "hard facts"; they are simply designed to suggest that zero economic growth and zero net environmental destruction may be two independent goals. A policy of zero economic growth makes no sense! A policy of zero net environmental destruction has much appeal. However, the rate of growth of GNP and the distribution of income depend on the package of policies chosen to implement zero net environmental destruction.

For a given rate of environmental destruction and a given inequality of income, there is a maximum rate of GNP growth which can be achieved through public policy. Society should select the combination of environmental destruction, income inequality, and economic growth which it deems most desirable.

Thurow is aware of these points. I was sorry that he did not consider the income distribution and environmental implications of the changed characteristics of the economy due to alternative zero economic-growth policies.

Thurow asserts that barring major institutional changes, zero economic growth would increase the inequality of income among whites, among blacks, and between whites and blacks. However, he dodges the important problem of distinguishing between temporary and permanent change and between cyclical and secular change. Does a given rate of growth of GNP have the same income-distribution implications regardless of whether it is permanent or temporary? Thurow concentrates on the short run. More than likely there would be a big difference in a long-run policy.

It was a common practice in time-series analyses of the inequality of income to use the unemployment rate as a proxy for labor-market conditions over the business cycle (Schultz, Metcalf, Thurow [1970]). However, it is the inequality of hours worked per year (or weeks worked per year) which is the appropriate analytical measure of the effect of the business cycle on the distribution of income. An example will clarify this. Suppose all workers earn the same weekly wage. In Year I, half of the workers work forty weeks and half work fifty-two weeks. There is income inequality, a dispersion in weeks worked, and unemployment. Let us assume that in Year II all workers are employed for only forty weeks. The inequality in weeks worked and in annual income is decreased to zero, yet unemployment has increased!

Thus, the relative inequality of hours worked per year and not the unemployment rate is the analytically correct variable to use in a study of the inequality of annual income. The unemployment rate is a good proxy for the relative inequality of hours worked over the business cycle only because employment declines relatively more during recessions at the lower employment levels, so that the relative inequality of hours worked increases.[4]

What will happen, however, to the relative inequality of hours worked and the unemployment rate for different groups if we take increases in productivity primarily as increases in leisure? This question is concerned with a secular rather than a cyclical change in labor-force behavior. If we use history as our guide, the average level of hours worked per year will decline, but neither the rate of unemployment nor the relative inequality of hours worked will increase.

The basic flaw in Thurow's analysis is his unwillingness to separate cyclical from secular changes. His basic assumption that the employment rate will decrease under ZEG at 3.1 percent per year generates his conclusion that zero economic growth implies greater income inequality. The problem stems from his using a regression equation designed to explain income inequality, but which does not explicitly include a "rate of change of GNP" variable. A recent international study (Chiswick 1971), which explicitly incorporated a "rate of growth of GNP per capita" variable, suggests that lower rates of economic growth result in a smaller inequality of income!

In summary, there are two basic reasons for my not being able to accept Thurow's conclusion that ZEG, unmodified by strong redistribution policies, will result in greater income inequality. First, he does not care to separate cyclical and secular changes in the distribution of employment. Second, other research which explicitly incorporates a rate of growth of GNP variable (under a ZNED policy) suggests that a lower rate of secular growth generates a smaller income inequality.

Notes

[1] Other relatively recent research on the effect of economic growth on the inequality of the income distribution can be found in Kuznets, Lydall, Chiswick (1971), and Chiswick and Mincer.

[2] According to this second view, we may have made some progress. It is my impression that the air in London, Pittsburgh, and several other cities is cleaner now than in past decades, and that the auto's replacing draft animals has made the streets, if not the air, in our urban centers far more pleasant.

[3] Technological advances in mineral extraction and transpor-

tation mean that real costs need not increase with the extraction of minerals.
[4] For the United States the unemployment rate is highly correlated with the inequality of weeks worked over the business cycle, but it is weakly correlated across states at a moment in time (Chiswick and Mincer, Hashimoto). In analyses of interstate differences in income inequality, Aigner and Heins used the unemployment rate and found it insignificant, while Chiswick (1972) found the relative inequality of weeks worked to have a significant positive effect.

References

Aigner, D. J. and Heins, A. J. "On the Determinants of Income Equality," *American Economic Review*, March 1967.

Chiswick, B. R. "Earnings Inequality and Economic Development," *Quarterly Journal of Economics*, February 1971.

Chiswick, B. R. "Inter-Regional Analyses of the Distribution of Income" (New York: National Bureau of Economic Research, mimeo, 1972).

Chiswick, B. R. and Mincer, J. "Time Series Changes in Personal Income Inequality in the United States from 1939, with Projections to 1985," *Journal of Political Economy*, Supplement, May/June 1972.

Hashimoto, M. "Factors Affecting State Unemployment," Ph.D. Dissertation, Columbia University, 1971.

Kuznets, S. "Quantitative Aspects of the Economic Growth of Nations: VIII Distribution of Income by Size," *Economic Development and Cultural Change*, January 1963.

Lydall, H. *The Structure of Earnings* (Oxford: The Clarendon Press, 1968).

Metcalf, C. E. "The Size Distribution of Personal Income During the Business Cycle," *American Economic Review*, September 1969.

Schultz, T. P. "Secular Trends and Cyclical Behavior of Income Distribution in the United States: 1944–1965," in *Six Papers on the Size Distribution of Wealth and Income* (New York: National Bureau of Economic Research, 1969).

Thurow, L. "Analyzing the American Income Distribution," *American Economic Review*, May 1970.

RICHARD A. EASTERLIN

The specifics of Lester Thurow's paper have been excellently discussed by Barry Chiswick. What I would like to do is use the Thurow paper as the basis for a few general remarks which seem to me to be appropriate to a symposium on problems of economic growth. Solow stressed in his presentation the need to distinguish the question of the possibility of growth from that of its desirability. I concur very much with his conclusion that economic growth is possible, the question to which he addressed himself. Indeed, I think both population growth and economic growth are possible. The problem that troubles me with regard to economic growth, however, has to do with the other issue, namely, its desirability. I can illustrate the problem by reference to Lester Thurow's comments on the relation of well-being to frequency of promotion. Thurow pointed out that in a zero economic-growth society, promotion might be much less frequent than in a rapidly growing society, implying that people are likely to be happier or more contented in a situation of frequent promotion, that is, of high upward mobility. But there is some evidence on this question which raises serious doubt about this implication. In a famous study of the American soldier in World War II, sociologist Samuel Stouffer compared the feelings of Air Corps men and military police with regard to promotion. The Air Corps had distinctly higher rates of promotion than the military police. In the Air Corps promotions were frequent and widespread, while among the MPs they were infrequent and very selective. It turned out that the members of the Air Corps were comparatively dissatisfied with the promotion situation, while among the MPs there was general satisfaction with the promotion setup, and much less feeling of frustration and anxiety. The reason for this was that the expectations of people regarding promotion differed between the two groups, and were influenced by their differing situations. In the Air Corps, where promotions were rapid, aspirations for promotions were very high. Those who were being promoted did not feel that they had accomplished very much, and those who were left behind felt they were being treated unfairly. Among the MPs, expectations of advancement were low. Those who were promoted were quite satisfied, and those who were not promoted did not feel mistreated, since generally very few received promotions.

In his comments, Thurow made reference to the prospects for promotion in his department at MIT. I think he can see the point I'm making from his own experience. The academic job market has gotten much tighter in recent years and the possibility of rapid promotion has generally diminished a great deal. My experience in talking to young prospects in recent years as compared with five to ten years ago is that the promotion aspirations of young men have been dampened quite a bit by this development. In other words, the aspirations for promotion have been altered by the objective conditions that young people are experiencing. As promotions become less frequent, the aspirations for promotion get scaled down.

I think these observations bear more generally on the question of economic growth. Economic growth means more goods. But the point I'm making is that the system within which one lives affects one's aspirations; and this relates to the question of what goods people want, just as much as to how rapidly they expect to get promoted. Hence people raised in richer societies tend to have correspondingly greater aspirations for goods. Let me give you a few examples of the kinds of goods aspirations in a country like India compared with a country like the United States, as reflected in replies to an open-ended question: "What would you need to make you happy?" (Hadley Cantril, *The Pattern of Human Concerns*, pp. 205–6, 221–2).

In India a thirty-year-old sweeper says, "I wish for an increase in my wages because with my meager salary I cannot afford to buy decent food for my family. If the food and clothing problems were solved, then I would feel at home and satisfied. Also, if my wife were able to work, the two of us could then feed the family; then I'm sure we would have a happy life and our worries would be over." A forty-five-year-old housewife in India says, "I should like a water-tap, a water supply in my house. It would also be nice to have electricity. My husband's wages must be increased if our children are to get an education and our daughter is to be married." A forty-year-old skilled worker says, "I hope in the future I will not get any disease. I also hope I can purchase a bicycle. I hope my children will study well and then I can provide them with an education. I also would sometime like to own a fan and maybe a radio."

Now here are some quotations from people in the United States: "I would like a reasonable-enough income to maintain a house, have a new car, have a boat and send my four children to private schools." That is a thirty-four-year-old laboratory technician. Another said, "I would like a new car. I wish all my bills were paid and I had more money for myself, and I would like to play more golf and to hunt more than I do. I would like to have more time to do the things I want to and to entertain my friends." That is the statement of a Negro bus driver. Finally, a twenty-eight-year-old lawyer said, "Materially speaking I would like to provide my family with an income to allow them to live well, to have the proper recreation, to go camping, to have music and dancing lessons for the children, and to have family trips. I wish we could belong to a country club, and do more entertaining. We have just bought a new home and expect to be perfectly satisfied with it for a number of years."

I submit that these remarks show clearly that the kinds of aspirations people form as to how they want to live are a product of their social experience. People who grow up in richer societies develop aspirations as to the way they should live and the kinds of goods they should have that are higher than those of people who grow up in poorer societies. In terms of formal economic analysis, what I am saying is that tastes are endogenous to economic growth and a positive function of the level of per capita income. As per capita income goes up, so too do the aspirations that people form.

If this is so, then it raises a serious question as to whether increases in income really make people any better off. Indeed, when one looks at results of studies of how happy people are in richer and poorer societies, they support the doubts raised by these observations. There is little or no evidence that people in poorer societies are less happy than people in richer societies, despite drastic differences in income. The principal reason is quite clear. Although people in richer societies have more, they want more, for their aspirations have been going up right along with the increase in their incomes.

This brings me back to the question of the desirability of economic growth. In the situation I have described, it seems to me that advocacy of economic growth becomes tantamount to committing society to a treadmill, to committing people year after year, generation after generation, to pursuing that which they can never attain—enough goods to make them happy. It seems to me that this is a serious problem which deserves recognition in discussions of economic growth, a problem quite different from the usual question of the technological feasibility of sustained growth.

10 | A dialogue on the issues

THE FOLLOWING dialogue is taken from the television program entitled "The Economic Growth Controversy," produced in conjunction with the Lehigh Symposium by the Lehigh Valley Educational Television Corporation, WLVT-TV, an affiliate of the National Education Television Network.

Professor Simon Rottenberg served as moderator of the discussion. The panelists were Professors Robert M. Solow, E. J. Mishan, Jay Anderson, and Finn B. Jensen.

MR. ROTTENBERG For the last two days we have been engaged in discussions on the problems of economic growth at a symposium at Lehigh University. This symposium has revealed itself to be a kind of adversary proceedings, in which two polar positions are taken. One is represented by Professor Solow. It takes the form that people are substantially better off in a material sense now than they were a century ago; and though this has produced costs in terms of pollution of the environment and the using up of scarce and unrenewable resources, those costs have been worthwhile. All things considered, we're better off than our forebears were.

The other polar case is represented by the position of Professor Mishan, who's not so sure that, all things considered, we're better off now than people were a century ago. And especially if one takes into account the threat to the environment and the persistence of nonrenewable resources in the future, there is a real threat to the survival of the community a century from now. So, in general, we have an optimistic point of view from Mr. Solow and a pessimistic point of view from Mr. Mishan. Perhaps we can begin our discussion with a few words from Mr. Solow.

MR. SOLOW   Well, behind the talk about the problem of economic growth is a set of attitudes and controversies and, just to get things started, let me just say what I think some of them are.

First, some people like modern life and others don't. Some of us, when we think of the way we live now, think mainly of conveniences that our parents and grandparents didn't have—like television, air conditioning, the possibility of traveling long distances quickly, and seeing places that we couldn't otherwise see. Others think mainly of crowding in cities, dirty air, dirty water, and things like that. Some of us like to contemplate the advance of science and the fact that we know more and more about the world we live in. Others worry mainly about the fact that you can't walk in the streets of some cities at night without running the risk of being mugged. So that's one difference of opinion in attitude that we have.

Second, it seems that some people are natural-born pessimists and other people are natural-born optimists. As Gilbert and Sullivan said, "Some people are born little liberals and others are born little conservatives." Either you think that every problem has a solution and people are clever enough, or ingenious enough, or lucky enough, so that they'll probably find it; or else you believe implicitly in the famous Murphy's Law: "Anything that can go wrong probably will go wrong."

Third, some people believe that we are already well on the way to exhausting our natural resources—exhausting the earth's capacity to carry a population and support life—and that we're doing it in a way that's bound to land us in a catastrophe of some kind, and probably pretty soon. Others, like me, believe that the forecasts of catastrophe—as horrible as they are—are probably wrong or simply not well based.

And, at the end, with all those differences of opinion, people differ very much on what a reasonable man should be worrying about; what every reasonable man should be wishing the world would do. Some of us think that what's necessary is to change very drastically the way we organize ourselves and the way we live; that we can't survive—people on earth can't survive—with any kind of decent standard of living unless something quite different and quite drastic happens to our economies, our governments, and our habits. Others, again like me, think that what a reasonable man should be worrying about are step-by-step improvements in the conditions of life; that it does make sense just to worry about tomorrow's water-and-air-pollution legislation. I take a good deal of pleasure in the fact that the Senate and the House overrode the President's veto of the water-pollution bill. Others, I suppose, think that that's a mere Band-aid on the modern world, and that the next time we take a shower it will wash off. I believe that it makes sense to try to improve transportation in large cities. I wish that the Congress had opened up the highway trust fund to mass transit because I think that would help make it easier for commuters like me to get in and out from their offices. Other people think that that's a mere palliative, not something that will have any lasting effects. And behind this discussion of that vague thing called economic growth, I think that's the sort of thing we're really talking about.

MR. ROTTENBERG Mr. Mishan, I don't know whether I should ask you to be responsive to what Mr. Solow says. Can you make the next comment?

MR. MISHAN Bob Solow said that some people are born optimists and some are born pessimists, but there's a category that chooses to be pessimists, and I'm one by choice, simply because, if you expect the worst, it usually turns out to be true and you're not disappointed.

I think we see eye to eye on a number of things —on the possibility of continued economic growth. Of course, he spoke only very briefly, but when I discussed this question, I brought up the possibility of several kinds of risks we are running through pursuing technology. Among the greatest dangers, of course, is a nuclear holocaust, simply because the knowledge of atomic power and nuclear war is spreading. Smaller countries now possess that potential. It's not impossible that some of the leaders of these smaller countries are fanatical. We could come to a sticky end that way.

I also mention the possibility of epidemics owing to continued travel; to genetic risks we're running simply by use of new chemicals, the long-term effects of which, singly or taken in combination, we cannot know for a long time. And perhaps when we do know, it will be too late. But quite aside from that, I think the question of whether we can count upon an unlimitable energy—which seems to be the key variable in the future—is still in doubt. I'd like to hear more about this; I don't regard myself as an expert on this factor. Again, on the Green Revolution, I still have doubts simply because it is a form of monoculture that is in itself very unstable in that it uses vast quantities of chemical pesticides and irrigation. So again, I think there is a question mark over that.

Quite apart from the possibility of continued

economic growth, there is the question of the consequences of economic growth, and there I think I go along
with Bob Solow. There are two sides to this. Until recently, of course, there was only one side. I'm glad to
see now that he recognizes that economic growth does
have costs. I am merely concerned with emphasizing
these costs. It's possible that I've overemphasized them,
and I'm willing to speculate about that. But the kinds I
did emphasize were not so much the familiar spillovers—
the pollutants, which I think we could cope with. I don't
say we will. I mean, if you're concerned with the future
of economic growth, you have to ask yourself about the
likelihood of government attacking this problem. I'm not
too optimistic there, so I leave that open.

But then there are the other consequences which
are unmeasurable, which seem to be inherent in the
processes of economic growth, and these I think are
wide open for discussion. I don't pose them as questions.
After all, growth is made possible by a spirit of ambition and motivation. It takes place in a system that breeds
discontent. If you're not discontent, you're not going to
struggle to improve your status. You're not going to
struggle to increase your consumption. And then I also
emphasize the possibility that the kinds of innovations
produced by economic growth—taking the form of effort-
saving, labor-saving devices—do in themselves reduce
contacts and some personal services. Examples are the
trend toward patient monitoring and hospital computer
diagnosis, closed-circuit television—all those things that
technology is now doing for people whereas before they
would have been directly in contact with one another,
doing the things themselves. Perhaps I had better rest
just for the moment.

MR. ROTTENBERG   Mr. Anderson, do you want to make a
comment?

MR. ANDERSON   I come from a background of the natural and physical sciences as opposed to the social sciences, and so when I think about the problems of growth I search my mind for examples in the natural sciences where I might find precedent. I'd like to share one particular example. There is a plateau near the Grand Canyon called the Kaibab Plateau. During the first decade of this century, there was a stable population of deer and mountain lion on the Kaibab Plateau. It then became possible to hunt mountain lions there, so that the limit to growth for the Kaibab deer rose very rapidly in the 1920s. But there is only so much sustenance on the Kaibab Plateau for deer and they overgrazed the plateau, exceeded the carrying capacity of their environment, and the population of deer fell precipitously. It has only been through very careful wildlife management over the rest of the century that the deer have returned to the normal state. Well, I think there are two features here that we can discuss. One is the notion of the carrying capacity of the environment—whether it is finite or not. And the second is the question of whether we will approach the carrying capacity of the environment so fast that our mechanisms for adapting to a new carrying capacity will be insufficiently rapid to catch up, and that we, too, will undergo some sort of overshoot and collapse.

Now, man isn't a deer; he is better than that. Man has evolved a set of social institutions which are designed to cope with just that kind of problem. The study group of which my wife and I were a part last year in the School of Management at MIT attempted to put together a formal model that would allow us to analyze just that kind of question—whether our societal mechanisms are rapid enough to allow us to adapt as we reach the carrying capacity of our environment. We came to the same conclusion that emerged in many of these wildlife situations: that they probably are not, and that the course for us might very well be an overshooting collapse of a similar nature.

MR. ROTTENBERG   Mr. Jensen?

MR. JENSEN   Well, I'll take off by talking about the social aspects. It seems as if the population of the world is pretty poor, most people are pretty poor and they look for work to progress. In underdeveloped countries working-class people—peasants—are looking for further growth and a higher standard of living. I think that's the reality. If we were to stop the growth, how would we stop it? How would we implement it? Through democratic processes? Hardly. Through a benevolent dictatorship? Such a thing doesn't exist, and I don't think we'd be interested in it. So I realize that there are dangers in the future. I'll confine myself to implementation. I think that in the United States we cope in some fashion with the problems as they come up. Yesterday I read in the *Wall Street Journal* about the stink near chemical factories, that the people living around them are up in arms and they'll be pressuring political leaders to pass legislation. I can give you an interesting example of this *ad hoc* approach, although it isn't the type of thing that can be done everywhere.

Recently, Norway was supposed to go into the Common Market and the political leaders were all in favor of it. Seventy-five percent of the elected parliament was in favor. Business leaders were in favor. The top labor leaders were in favor. But the man on the street was not because he likes to sail, he likes to hike, he likes the waterfalls.

The right to establishment, as it's called in the Common Market states, affirms that any Common Market country can locate in any other Common Market country. The people foresaw utilization of the waterfalls for power, a chemical industry, pollution of the fjords, and it just wasn't worth it. They decided collectively, in a democratic fashion, that it wasn't worth it.

I don't think that can be done in underdeveloped countries because people are poor. In India, for example, they die from things like malaria. I would say that if I were an Indian father with five kids and I saw malaria all around, I would be in favor of DDT. Very much so. It may pollute—in our country we'd say that's bad—but a democratic India would be in favor of DDT.

MR. ROTTENBERG What's not clear to me, in fact, is whether we have reached a meeting of the minds. That is to say, do we all believe that if economic growth came at zero cost, it would be a good thing? We all know that it doesn't come at zero cost. Have we reached consensus that, in fact, we ought to keep growth rates in check because it doesn't come at zero cost, because there are adverse side effects for additional increments of business services produced? Are there still differences among us?

MR. SOLOW I think there are probably still differences among us, but one can't really state it that way. There's almost nothing good that comes without some side effects. There's always a kind of net balance to be struck, and Finn's remark about DDT is a perfectly clear example of that. Nobody believes that malaria is a good thing. Nobody believes that the kind of poisoning of the food chain that excessive use of DDT causes is a good thing. For us—I mean, people in relatively rich countries like the United States and Japan, and most of Western Europe—it's pretty clear where the balance lies. Malaria has more or less been eradicated long ago. We can do without DDT. We're rich enough to find less dangerous substitutes. But in poor countries like India —tropical countries generally—it's not that people kid themselves that DDT is harmless. They've weighed the balance of benefits and costs and decided that it's worthwhile going ahead. And I must say that I'm with Finn in that I couldn't see it otherwise if I tried to put myself in their shoes.

MR. ROTTENBERG   Is this something that you find acceptable, Mr. Mishan—that there are circumstances in which environmentally polluting agents would be a good thing because more good comes out of their use than the harm that they do?

MR. MISHAN   Yes, that's also valid of course for affluent countries as well. This is part of the traditional doctrine. I don't have any quarrel with that on a purely formal level. But when you address yourself to continued economic growth in affluent countries like the United States, I think it's legitimate for those people who support it to recognize the possible consequences—the risk one has to take. What is it they regard as the goods in this thing? It's very hard to see this. You see, are you alleging that, on the average, Americans are happy today—happier than they were in 1950, happier than they were in, say, 1929; or are they happier than they are in Britain, where the standard of living is roughly half that of the U. S.? If you believe you cannot make such a statement, why do you persist in it? I mean, I could take this a bit further, but I'd like to hear Bob Solow on this.

MR. SOLOW   Well, I have no way of knowing any more than Ed does that people are happier now than they were in 1950. I can speak for myself—I am happier now than I was in 1950. I can't remember 1929, but I can remember 1934 and 1935 when my father was unemployed. I think I am happier now than he was then; and probably happier than I was then to the extent that I knew what my parents were worrying about. I rather like a lot of things I do now that I couldn't do in 1950 or 1945 or 1948 because I'm better off now. A lot of people aren't as well off as I am. But I have very little hesitation about that. Now, there's a deep sense in which I suppose no one has any way of knowing whether people are any happier now than they were in the Middle Ages, i.e., the cheerful peasant. I have my suspicions about that, but I would certainly never claim that I could prove it.

MR. ROTTENBERG   Well, I take it, Mr. Mishan, that when you ask whether people are happier now than they were in times when material standards of life were lower, you're already suggesting that you think they're not happier. Is that correct? Because if this were so, it only suggests that the basket of commodities and services we're producing in larger and larger quantities per unit of time, as time passes, is the wrong basket of goods and services. If you believe some other basket of goods and services would produce happiness, then that is what we ought to be producing instead. It doesn't say that we ought not to grow; we ought simply to have a different composition of goods and services being produced.

MR. MISHAN   Well, that only meets it part of the way. It's quite true that as you get wealthier you can afford to dispense with more material goods and go in for more environmental goods. I'll go along with that. But when I'm criticizing growth as a process, I think more in terms of technology. Is the process of technology itself somewhat corrupting to the human spirit? Is it corrosive? Now, of course, I know that in all times there have been avarice and greed. But not in all times were they regarded as a virtue and transmuted into motivation and ambition, which are good things. The question then is: Once man is possessed of this spirit, once there's an ethos of cultivated discontent, can't that interfere very much with his sense of enjoyment?

MR. JENSEN   Well, I'd say that if we go back a couple of generations, college professors may have been relatively better off with their smaller incomes than they are today. The well-to-do were relatively better off, but as for the masses of the American people, I just can't see that they were better off. The long hours in coal mines! With technological progress, coal mining is less dangerous; it's still dangerous, but it's less unpleasant. The steel workers had workdays of ten—go back far enough, twelve—hours. Certainly these people must be better off today. And I think it's silly to be cynical about such people using snowmobiles, motorcycles, and that type of thing, rather than reading poetry. That's a value judgment. They enjoy themselves much more I'm sure, so I'm positive on that. They enjoy themselves much more than they did with the drudgery of a twelve-hour day. Technology has brought this about.

MR. ROTTENBERG   Your proposition, Mr. Mishan, seems to take the form that the quantity of happiness is inverse to the material conditions of life.

MR. MISHAN   No. We are talking about countries that are already past subsistence levels, that are fairly comfortable. Assuming certain abuses, which Mr. Jensen mentioned, have been overcome—obviously I wouldn't oppose making mines more comfortable, or less risky, or reducing hours—what I'm concerned about is whether from now on, having achieved a certain standard of living, or take the last two or three decades, are we really on the right path? Are we really moving forward in any meaningful sense? I don't think you can make a distinction, incidentally, between welfare and happiness. To me, they're synonymous terms. And neither can you measure economic welfare and happiness. So with contentment, I mean, are people becoming more contented? Now, one of the things which Professor Solow brought up was the new options open to people today, and I think he cited travel in this connection. But, again, I think he'll agree with me that it has a cost, perhaps enormous. In this process of travel, package tourism has irrevocably been destroying a whole heritage of natural beauty on an unprecedented scale. I have been traveling through the Mediterranean, year after year, looking for a quiet spot and seeing what has happened all over the coastline of the Mediterranean—the waters polluted, the scenery gone, cement hotels everywhere. Now, of course, Bob Solow will say, "Yes, but that's all right. People want this sort of thing." But there are two things here as well. First of all, it's like any other problem in economics. It has spillover effects. It may not be easily measurable, but it can be terribly important. And the second thing is that the cost falls largely on the future generations. We're not opening it up; we're actually closing it to them. We don't have to depend only on package tourism for that. The automobile itself is perhaps the greatest destroyer of natural beauty and of cities that I can think of. In England, for example, population hasn't increased that much between 1950 and 1970, possibly by about five million. Yet during that time urban areas have spread out. What was once beautiful countryside has disappeared. I know people say this is an elitist argument, but what it really means is that *nobody* can enjoy it, not even the elites. And it is also not the point, as I think Professor Kranzberg noted, that these things have been said before. You can go back to the age of Chaucer and people will be lamenting the loss of the countryside. And you go on through the eighteenth century and they're still lamenting it, and they'll lament even more today.

MR. SOLOW   I'm with Ed on the automobile. I'm no great lover of the automobile and I think one has to find ways of controlling it. But it still isn't clear to me for whom we're saving the countryside. I get very little pleasure from knowing that the countryside is there if I can't see it. I get not much more pleasure thinking that if I don't see it, somebody else in a hundred years will be able to see it. I do think it matters that people do in fact choose to visit the Riviera. If I ski at Killington in Vermont with thousands of other people, I could wish that there were only half as many people on those lifts, but I would resent it if I were one of the half that couldn't go.

MR. MISHAN   Yes, but you'd resent it even more if there were no skiing at all.

I think a fair standard of living had been achieved in the United States by the turn of the century, certainly by the 1920s, and also in Britain. If you're going to make comparisons, I think they're the reasonable kind of comparison. That's where my doubts lie about the advantages of living now as against thirty years ago or fifty years ago.

But I would never support the zero-growth position. I'm not a zero economic-growth man because, in fact, if we could measure some standard of human contentment, we'd find out that we've been on the negative-growth path a lot already. Therefore, if you suggested that we have to have a zero rate of growth, we should probably react with accelerated economic growth, which is what I don't want. All I am saying is that there are other criteria and, having reached a certain level of affluence, we should look into them. As for persuading the individual consumer, all one can do is begin with a minority position. This is the democratic process. At first you meet with ridicule, gradually you make an impression, and bit by bit the movement grows. I couldn't do it single-handedly. I couldn't expect to. I'm not putting myself in the position of a dictator. I'm saying that we should discuss these matters and persuade people that economic growth is not going to give them what they imagine it's going to give them. If you can persuade them, then the question of how to do it and the consequences of making the transition could be dealt with more sensibly. But we've first got to persuade people of this.

MR. JENSEN   I believe it would also mean the redistribution of income.

MR. MISHAN   Yes, that's what I regard as one of the good features.

MR. SOLOW   What attitude do you take to the billions of people in the world who live essentially at a subsistence level now? What's your message to India, Pakistan, Bengal, Latin America, and Southeast Asia?

MR. MISHAN   You know, of course, this is something I always avoid if I can. I always find myself in affluent America or Europe. If you press me, I'll just very tentatively say to them: "Don't take the Western path. If you want to take any path, take the path that Ghandi outlined: intermediate technology. Learn to be satisfied with little. It can be done. It has been done for centuries." I think that's about all I would say.

MR. ROTTENBERG   If somebody should ask you: What about those who are nonaffluent, who indeed are quite poor, but in the affluent countries? Would you say the same thing? Learn to be content.

MR. MISHAN   For Americans it would be more embarrassing because it turns out that the poverty level is a little above the average standard of living in Britain. With a certain sense of mortification, I have to admit this. I think the hard-core poverty in Britain works out to be about eight million people. That's men, women, and children. The amount they would need could be given from a small growth in British GNP. It could be done by redistributive measures. Now, before Bob Solow steps in and says "Unrealistic," he doesn't have to. I'm the first to say it's unrealistic. But the fact that it's not realistic is what I regard as a condemnation of economic growth itself. It's not possible even in the United States now. Yet the standard of living here is five times as high as it was in Britain about 1950, when we had just come out of the war and the rationing was still on. And in this country we just can't see the possibility of trying to improve the wretched poverty of a few million people because you just seem to need that extra money. This is one of the worst condemnations of economic growth because I can see no end to it. I mean, you can go into a century hence and you'll still have poverty and you still won't be able to equalize because you'll say it's just politically impossible. People just won't wear it. And that, I say, is the ethos of technology.

11 | The club of rome model

W. E. SCHIESSER

THE MATHEMATICAL modeling and computer analysis of economic and social systems, epitomized by the Club of Rome world model, has developed rapidly in the last decade. This activity, which has arisen because of the need to better understand the evolution of our complex, highly structured society, has become possible with the availability of powerful computers which provide solutions to large, complex mathematical models. However, until recently the quantitative analysis of economic and social systems has been essentially limited to studies of segments of society, such as the operations of a corporation, the growth and decay of an urban area, or the development of a particular industry. The Club of Rome model is the first attempt to analyze the evolution of the entire world system. The model provides long-term projections of such major factors as world population, pollution, per capita food supply, natural resource utilization, and capital investment. The model and its computer output have received widespread comment, both favorable and unfavorable. Much of the reaction has been based on an incomplete understanding of the model and how it generates numerical results.*

---

* The author has available a FORTRAN IV computer program for the global model which can be executed on essentially any computer if one wishes to obtain an in-depth understanding of the model.

The availability of computers was a prerequisite for the development of the Club of Rome model because the model equations are sufficiently complex and nonlinear so that they cannot be solved by analytical methods that one might use, for example, to solve a set of linear algebraic equations. Rather, a numerical step-by-step procedure is used to compute the time-evolution of variables such as the world's population and per capita food supply. Furthermore, since all of the major variables of the model are interrelated in a complex structure, the complete set of equations must be solved simultaneously. Consequently, the number of numerical operations required to move the model through time is very large and can only be done practically through the use of a computer.

With this in mind, perhaps it would be helpful here to provide a brief historical perspective of the Club of Rome model and to discuss some of the output of the global model.

The Club of Rome is a group of internationally prominent individuals who have met informally since 1968 to discuss what they consider to be certain alarming developments in the world today. Specifically, the Club of Rome is interested in the analysis of the evolving world system and especially such trends as the growing world population and level of pollution, the depletion of natural resources, and the need for an ever-increasing food supply. In order to obtain a better overall perspective of these trends, the Club of Rome commissioned Professor Jay W. Forrester of MIT to undertake a quantitative analysis of the world system. In particular, the Club sought a comprehensive analysis which would include the interaction of all major factors which affect the evolving world system. This approach was new at the time and stood in contradistinction to the piecemeal approach which had characterized quantitative economic model-building up to that time.

Professor Forrester was eminently qualified to undertake such a study since he had pioneered the field of "systems dynamics" in which mathematical modeling and computer simulation are applied to the quantitative analysis of complex systems. Forrester's analysis resulted in a preliminary model, generally termed World 2, which is thoroughly described and documented in his book *World Dynamics*.* World 2 contains as the major worldwide outputs: (1) population, (2) pollution level, (3) level of natural resources, (4) total capital investment, (5) capital investment in agriculture, and (6) "quality of life." The latter is an arbitrarily defined quantity which essentially reflects human well-being in terms of a composite of material standards, food supply, crowding and pollution.

The World 2 model is highly simplified, is based essentially on assumed relationships (rather than relationships based on data), and is highly aggregated (i.e., no attempt is made, for example, to distinguish between segments of the world's population on the basis of the relative availability of capital, wealth, etc.). These features of the model have all been the basis for criticism. However, the model is the first of its kind and therefore can be viewed as a pioneering effort that should be refined and extended to increase its realism and reliability with respect to the accuracy of the long-term projections.

There has been much criticism of the model. But critics should realize that the initial effort to model the world system should logically be limited in detail so that it can be implemented with reasonable effort and

---

*The World 2 model and the summary of Forrester's conclusions which follow are reprinted with permission of Wright-Allen Press, Inc., Cambridge, Mass.

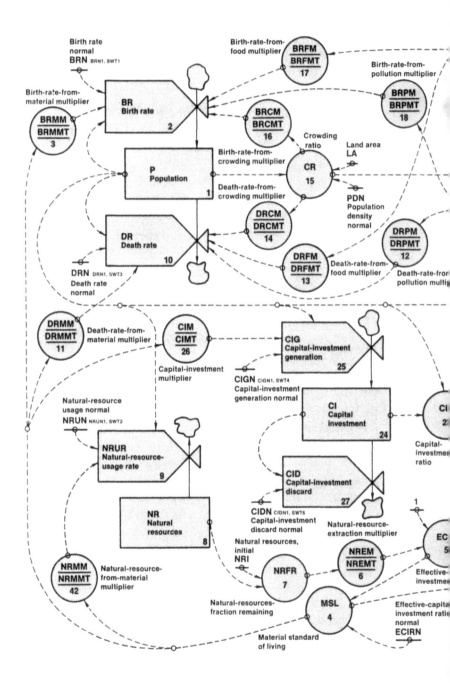

Figure 1: Block Diagram of the Structure of the World 2 Model

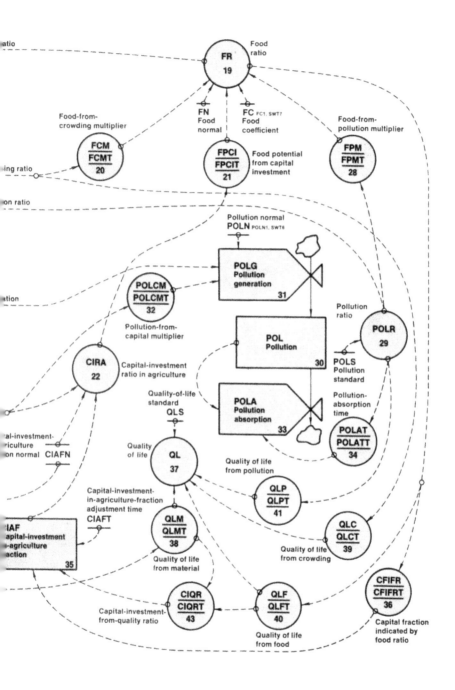

atio

FR
19
Food ratio

Food-from-crowding multiplier

FCM / FCMT
20

ing ratio

on ratio

FN
Food normal

FC FC1, SWT7
Food coefficient

FPCI / FPCIT
21
Food potential from capital investment

Food-from-pollution multiplier

FPM / FPMT
28

Pollution normal
POLN POLN1, SWT6

ation

POLCM / POLCMT
32
Pollution-from-capital multiplier

POLG
Pollution generation
31

CIRA
22
Capital-investment ratio in agriculture

Pollution ratio

POLR
29

POL
Pollution
30

POLS
Pollution standard

Quality-of-life standard
QLS

POLA
Pollution absorption
33

Pollution-absorption time

POLAT / POLATT
34

al-investment-riculture
on normal CIAFN

Quality of life

QL
37

Quality of life from pollution

QLP / QLPT
41

QLC / QLCT
39
Quality of life from crowding

Capital-investment-in-agriculture-fraction adjustment time
CIAFT

QLM / QLMT
38
Quality of life from material

IAF
apital-investment -agriculture action
35

CIQR / CIQRT
43
Capital-investment-from-quality ratio

QLF / QLFT
40
Quality of life from food

CFIFR / CFIFRT
36
Capital fraction indicated by food ratio

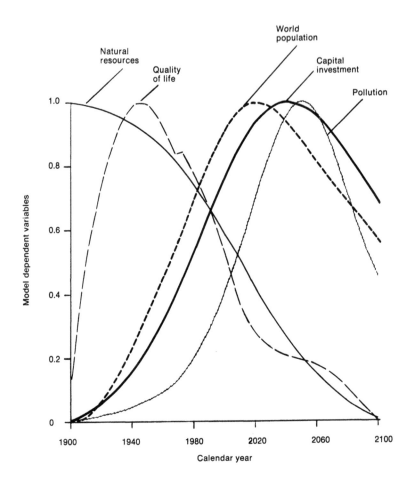

Figure 2. Response of the World 2 Model with the Depletion of Natural Resources

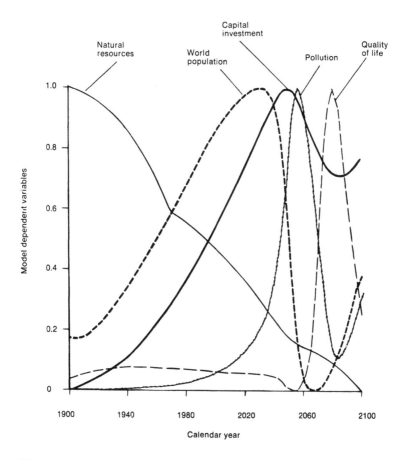

Figure 3. Response of the World 2 Model for the Pollution Crisis Case:
Depletion of Natural Resources Rate Reduced by 75 Percent
Relative to Figure 2

the results can be obtained within a reasonable period of time. If the initial results are judged to be interesting and worthwhile, there is justification for additional work. Clearly, it would be difficult to attempt to model in detail every aspect of the world system, since much of the required information is unavailable; moreover, such a rigorous requirement would make even the initial results impossible to achieve. To reason by analogy, one could argue that Henry Ford's first car should have looked like the Ford cars which now roll off the assembly line. Obviously it required many years of research and development before the industry learned how to build today's cars. Similarly, continuing development of the global model will be required to give it essential detail and realism.

Another point of criticism (and also a source of confusion) is the fact that two global models have been discussed in the open literature. Professor Meadows and a group of co-workers, also at MIT, extended the Forrester model. The output of this model, called World 3, forms the basis of the much publicized book *The Limits to Growth*. Unfortunately, the technical details of World 3 are described quite superficially in *The Limits to Growth*. The situation is analogous to one in which a scientist reports a series of experimental results without indicating how the results were obtained. Other scientists who are interested in the work cannot verify the reported results by repeating the experiments or extend the results through additional research. The technical details (i.e., the equations) of the World 3 model are still not available in the open literature.

The structure of a relatively detailed global model consists of a complex interconnection of "feedback loops." For example, the World 2 model, illustrated in Figure 1, consists of five level variables represented by rectangles, which are population (P, no. 1), natural resources (NR, no. 8), capital investment (CI, no. 24), pollution (POL, no. 30) and capital-investment-in-agriculture-fraction (CIAF, no. 35). The interconnecting feedback loops define the rate variables which are the input to or output from the valve-shaped blocks. The circles represent specific functional relationships that define the rates.

A detailed discussion of Figure 1 is not possible here, and it is presented primarily to indicate the complexity of the model. One can say, however, that the information and predictions generated by the model yield little hope for continuing increases in our present standard of living beyond the year 2100. Indeed, many disamenities begin to show themselves much sooner. Figure 2, for example, is a graphic depiction which shows the "quality of life" steadily declining in the future, the decline resulting from the depletion of natural resources. Figure 3, however, depicts a model which assumes that the rate at which natural resources are used up can be reduced, and that the decline in the "quality of life" is not as precipitous.

The two examples of the model output in Figures 2 and 3 are not isolated cases, but rather are typical of the serious degradation or total collapse of the world system as projected by the model. Generally, whenever one source of pressure which causes worldwide catastrophe is relieved, another source develops, usually a relatively short time later, to also cause eventual collapse. This general mode of response of the World 2 model has been summarized by Forrester in *World Dynamics* (pp. 11-13) :

1. Industrialization may be a more fundamental disturbing force in world ecology than is population. In fact, the population explosion is perhaps best viewed as a result of technology and industrialization. (Medicine and public health are included here as a part of industrialization.)

2. Within the next century, man may face choices from a four-pronged dilemma—suppression of modern industrial society by a natural-resource shortage; decline of world population from changes wrought by pollution; population limitation by food shortage; or population collapse from war, disease, and social stresses caused by physical and psychological crowding.

3. We may now be living in a "golden age" when, in spite of a widely acknowledged feeling of malaise, the quality of life is, on the average, higher than ever before in history and higher now than the future offers.

4. Exhortations and programs directed at population control may be inherently self-defeating. If population control begins to result, as hoped, in higher per capita food supply and material standard of living, these very improvements may relax the pressures and generate forces to trigger a resurgence of population growth.

5. The high standard of living of modern industrial societies seems to result from a production of food and material goods that has been able to outrun the rising population. But, as agriculture reaches a space limit, as industrialization reaches a natural-resource limit, and as both reach a pollution limit, population tends to catch up. Population then grows until the "quality of life" falls far enough to stabilize population.

6. There may be no realistic hope of the present underdeveloped countries reaching the standard of living demonstrated by the present industrialized nations. The pollution and natural-resource load placed on the world environmental system by each person in an advanced country is probably 20 to 50 times greater than the load now generated by a person in an underdeveloped country. With 4 times as many people in underdeveloped countries as in the present developed countries, their rising to the economic level that has been set as a standard by the industrialized nations could mean an increase of 10 times in the natural-resource and pollution load on the world environment. Noting the destruction that has already occurred on land, in the air, and especially in the oceans, capability appears not to exist for handling such a rise in standard of living. In fact, the present disparity between the developed and

underdeveloped nations may be equalized as much by a decline in the developed countries as by an improvement in the underdeveloped countries.

7. A society with a high level of industrialization may be nonsustainable. It may be self-extinguishing if it exhausts the natural resources on which it depends. Or, if unending substitution for declining natural resources were possible, a new international strife over pollution and environmental rights might pull the average world-wide standard of living back to the level of a century ago.

8. From the long view of a hundred years hence, the present efforts of underdeveloped countries to industrialize may be unwise. They may now be closer to an ultimate equilibrium with the environment than are the industrialized nations. The present underdeveloped countries may be in a better condition for surviving forthcoming world-wide environmental and economic pressures than are the advanced countries. If one of the several forces strong enough to cause a collapse in world population does arise, the underdeveloped countries might suffer far less than their share of the decline because economies with less organization, integration, and specialization are probably less vulnerable to disruption.

These pessimistic conclusions are clearly tied to the potential problems of unrestricted growth. The Club of Rome report, embodied in the quantitative studies of Forrester and Meadows, has dramatically called these problems to the attention of the world society. Much additional research now remains to be done. The models must be developed and refined to improve their reliability. Nevertheless, if the principal results remain essentially unaltered, we must face their critical economic, sociological and ecological implications for the future world society.

For Product Safety Concerns and Information please contact our EU
representative GPSR@taylorandfrancis.com
Taylor & Francis Verlag GmbH, Kaufingerstraße 24, 80331 München, Germany

www.ingramcontent.com/pod-product-compliance
Ingram Content Group UK Ltd.
Pitfield, Milton Keynes, MK11 3LW, UK
UKHW020935180425
457613UK00019B/404